My Faith Is Taking Me Someplace

Are You on the Road to Nowhere?

BY ANDREW MERRITT

CREATION HOUSE
Orlando, FL

MY FAITH IS TAKING ME SOMEPLACE by Andrew Merritt
Published by Creation House
Strang Communications Company
600 Rinehart Road, Lake Mary, Florida 32746
Web site: http://www.creationhouse.com

Unless otherwise noted, all Scripture quotations are from the King
James Version of the Bible.

Scripture quotations marked THE MESSAGE are from
THE MESSAGE, The New Testament in Contemporary Language
Copyright © 1993 by Eugene H. Peterson, Navpress.
Used by permission.

Scripture quotations marked NAS are from the New American
Standard Bible. Copyright © 1960, 1962, 1963, 1968, 1971, 1972,
1973, 1975, 1977 by the Lockman Foundation. Used by permission.

Scripture quotations marked NKJV are from the New King
James Version of the Bible. Copyright © 1979, 1980, 1982 by
Thomas Nelson Inc., publishers. Used by permission.

Copyright © 1997 by Andrew Merritt
All rights reserved
Library of Congress Catalog Card Number: 97-65689
ISBN: 0-88419-458-2

Printed in the United States of America

8901234 BBG 87654

To my children—
Anita, April, Rachelle,
Laura, Jonathan, and David—

AND TO MY GRANDCHILDREN—
Haki, Kirkland, and Mariah.

ACKNOWLEDGMENTS

Creating a book like this one is rarely accomplished through the efforts of a single individual. God uses many special people to help an author to discover truth, refine it, and put it into a form that will bless and help others.

I am grateful to the wonderful congregation at Straight Gate Church in Detroit, Michigan, who listened to and faithfully received the messages that became the body of this work. Without their love, prayers, and encouragement, this book would not have been possible.

Bishop T. D. Jakes, whom I respect and love as my pastor and friend in Christ, also helped make this book a reality. In addition to his counsel and encouragement, the initial contact with Creation House to publish *My Faith Is Taking Me Someplace* occurred on an occasion when Bishop Jakes had graciously allowed me to serve him.

I am also appreciative to Jim Kerby, whose editorial assistance was invaluable, and to Steve Strang and the wonderful people at Creation House who believed in me.

Most of all, I acknowledge the long, loving, patient support of my dear wife, Viveca, who even understood when I spent many hours of our precious vacation time finishing up the project.

I pray that the same presence and Spirit of God that was upon me as I wrote will be with you as you read this book and discover that, indeed, your faith is taking you someplace!
—ANDREW MERRITT
DETROIT, MICHIGAN

CONTENTS

FOREWORD

THE KEY to your chariot awaits you as you read *My Faith Is Taking Me Someplace*. You are about to set out on a voyage that will stop only when you reach the place for which you were created to occupy.

This kind of book is not for "couch-potato" Christians who want to live within their comfort zones. This is combustible theology that, mixed with the passion of prayer, will detonate in the homes and hearts of all who touch these sacred truths. Suddenly we realize that faith is not a destination; it is a vehicle that transports the faith-filled to their destinies.

There is a place that you have been called to reach. It

is a place that you cannot reach on foot. That's right—it will not be by foot. It will be *by faith*. The only way to scale the walls and bridge the gaps is to do it *by faith*. Have you noticed that the words *by faith* are scattered all over the eleventh chapter of Hebrews? It is said that men like Enoch, Abel, Moses, Abraham, and many others moved, worked, and survived *by faith*. The words *by faith* tell you how they did what they did so that you and I might better understand how we are to be transported into the next realm of glory.

The most threatening question that is being whispered in the hearts today of many professing believers is probably never even voiced. That question simply asks, "What is real faith?" In these times, many have confused the power with the anointing that accompanies real faith. Even secular nonbelievers have coined clichés like "keep the faith." There seems to be a popular connotation to the term *faith* that merely assigns it to mental attitude rather than spiritual conviction. The message that is taught in Scripture has become weakened by humanistic concepts associated with positive thinking, mind power, and other notions. These ideas, though noble in design, were spawned through the diluted pairing of Christian concepts with psychological jargon.

Sadly, these mutated distortions which are the off-spring of psychology and theology have replaced in the minds of many the real potency that comes from hearts that have faith in God. The mandate that Jesus set forth for His disciples was simple, specific, and clear. He told them to *have faith in God.* There is a vast difference between a heart that has *faith in faith* and one that has *faith in God.* The deterioration of this pure teaching has led to the demise of abundant living in the hearts of many Christians who have failed to draw a line of distinction between the legitimate and the illegitimate use of the term *faith.*

We find ourselves, therefore, in the midst of these tangled webs of concepts that are often spun in the minds of crafty men who desire to find a way to adapt the sanctity of the Christian message into compromising, mediocre reasoning that might win the approval of carnal men. It takes a lot of courage to resist the temptation to try to win the accolades of others. Some of us would rather preach the truth of God. It is amid the scoffing of many that God raises up a few individuals in each generation who light the torch that leads His children away from the Egyptian mentality of sin and into the milk and honey of fulfilled promise. In fact, in this time of massive challenges and unusual crises, we are commanded, as Jude would say, to "earnestly [contend] for the faith that was once delivered unto the saints" (v. 3).

We understand that real, uncut, concentrated faith is so potent that it will impregnate the converted with hope and infuse hearts with a sense of the divine presence of God. The faith that transcends all barriers and reaches all intellects is so transforming that Satan has done all he could do to hide the glorious faith-producing gospel from shining into human hearts. Alas, he is defeated again, for even in this present time, God is releasing those who have the kind of bodacious faith that is too radical to be thwarted into silence.

There is an obvious journey taking place in the body of Christ. It is the exodus of our generation. We are leaving the slave plains of our captivity. We have turned over our brick and mortar, and we are answering the challenge to follow God.

I can hear a trumpet blowing in Zion. It is a blaring sound that pierces depression and despair. It has called us out, and we cannot go back in. We are assembling our forces and rallying our strength.

This book is filled with torch-lighting, fire-igniting, direction that God has reserved for men and women who are ready to break through the secular into the supernatural. It is a graphic depiction of the Holy Spirit's ability to deliver us from one destination to another by the power of His Word. As you read, your traditions may cringe, your excuses may scream. You may even find yourself so challenged that you pack your bags and move from the mundane beaches of frolic and frivolity into the brigade of marching feet of an army that is not on vacation but in hot pursuit of the things God has promised.

There is a hot molten lava cascading down the heart of Andrew Merritt, and it is burning everything in its path. I can assure you that this consuming fire is going to bring about an undisputed change.

As you read his book, it will challenge you to leave the ranks of men whose faith is merely a dormant creed of ethics noted in a mausoleum of books and documents. It will challenge you to become a part of the thriving, volcano-type faith that erupts with tumultuous reverberations and alters whatever it touches.

Warning! This book is not for the faint or the foolish. Faith is a subject for giant-killing men who know they have the weapons needed to fight the opposition. If we aspire toward the call of God, this word will become the petroleum that oils our hearts and ignites our dreams. It is time to burn. It is time to allow our vision to catch flame in our own spirits. It is time to take back what the enemy has stolen. Our slavery is over. We are kings and priests unto God.

This book is a compass that Bishop Merritt has placed firmly into the hands of people who have a directional pull toward the purpose and destiny of the Lord. I have watched this message incubate in Bishop Merritt's heart and I have seen the fruit of it evidenced in his own life. Every person around him can see the results of faith and vision embodied in his thriving ministry, his abundant blessing, and his consecration toward God. Ladies and gentlemen, without further *adieu,* I present to you the voice of the Lord etched on these pages. It is crisp, it is clean, and it is timely. I should only hesitate long enough to advise you to read every word with your bags packed and your car running. Because no matter where you were spiritually when you start reading, when all is said and done, you will drive wildly into your promise, exclaiming, *"My faith is taking me someplace!"*

—BISHOP T. D. JAKES, SR.
DALLAS, TEXAS

INTRODUCTION

FAITH—God has given each of us a measure of it. And real faith—the God-kind of faith—will cause us to take God-ordered steps that are taking us someplace.

Is your faith taking you someplace? Or do you feel as if you were on the road to nowhere? Maybe your job is a dead end . . . or you wish you were married but can't find the right person . . . or you're just tired of the way you're living your life.

Are you living in poverty and need, frustrated by unfulfilled ambitions? Are you tormented by worry, fear, and the cares of this life? Is your heart dead and cold toward God?

The Bible provides many great object lessons on how faith works—numerous accounts of people who set out to obtain the unobtainable by following God's instructions with unquestioning faith, refusing to be defeated. From them, we learn that faith has a destination, and that faith must be determined and persistent.

When we really believe that God can do the impossible—and that He is able and willing to do so—we can learn to trust Him in any situation or circumstance. We learn to overcome fear, knowing that God is working in the middle of our messes, and that He is always near.

Faith always moves forward—never backing up or turning around. Faith doesn't always follow man's rules, and does not resign itself to particular conditions. Only the slave mentality of people who are bound by their own attitudes can shortcircuit faith.

Because faith pleases God, Satan wants to steal it and render us ineffective in the Kingdom of God. But God provided redemption for mankind by sending His Son to destroy the works of the devil. Jesus is our example, and He showed us that faith is the key to being a productive servant of God.

The promise found in Isaiah 54:17—"No weapon that is formed against thee shall prosper"—is the heritage of the servants of the Lord. Notice that it doesn't say "no weapon will be formed against" us. Rather, it says the weapons will not be successful. The key to having no weapon succeed against you is to serve the Lord and live by faith.

If your faith isn't taking you someplace, it needs to be reactivated. Faith is the victory that makes you an overcomer. It is the key to positive changes in your life. Commit your ways unto the Lord and trust Him to know what's best for you.

God has given us faith—but faith has its price. It will take you straight to the heart of danger, into the presence of your enemies, and through the valley of the shadow of death.

Jesus' faith took Him to Gethsemane . . . to Golgotha . . . to the cross.

John's faith took him into exile on the lonely Isle of Patmos.

Peter's faith took him to an upside-down cross outside Jerusalem.

Paul's faith took him to Rome, to be beheaded on Nero's chopping block.

But their faith didn't fail them. Their faith took them *to* death, *through* death . . . and beyond.

Where is your faith taking you?

—BISHOP ANDREW MERRITT
DETROIT, MICHIGAN

CHAPTER ONE

FAITH ON THE MOVE

F AITH! Everybody talks about it. Ministers preach sermons about it. The library is full of books written about it. Churches, schools, and entire religious movements call themselves by its name. The Bible refers to it scores of times.

What is it? How do you describe and define it? The dictionary says *faith* is "firm belief in something for which there is no proof; belief and trust in and loyalty to God."

The Bible's famous faith chapter, Hebrews 11, says, "Now faith is the substance of things hoped for, the evidence of things not seen" (11:1).

Eugene Peterson, in his shopping-mall, street-language version of the Scriptures called *The MESSAGE,* translates the verse this way: "The fundamental fact of existence is that this trust in God, this faith, is the firm foundation under everything that makes life worth living. It's our handle on what we can't see." I'm told that the Bible contains several thousand precious promises of God that are available to His people who can utilize faith to access them. "If you believe," God says, "you can receive."

Where does faith come from? It is not an invention of man, not simply a part of the human personality. Faith is a product of God, and emanates or flows out from Him. Faith is given to us primarily to carry out the purpose of creation. Mankind was created for God's pleasure, for His honor and glory. We were not created for our independent, self-centered existence. We were made in His likeness, to be His companions, to have fellowship with God!

"But without faith," the Bible says, "it is impossible to please him: for he that cometh to God must believe that he is, and that he is a rewarder of them that diligently seek him" (Heb. 11:6). So faith is not optional. It is not an elective, an extra. It is essential, a necessity, a matter of life and death. Faith is vital to our well being.

How do we get faith? Man did not invent it. We cannot manufacture it. And it is available from only one source. God gives it to us. The apostle Paul declared that "God hath dealt to every man the measure of faith" (Rom. 12:3). He also said, "For by grace are ye saved *through faith;* and that not of yourselves: *it is the gift of God:* not of works, lest any man should boast" (Eph. 2:8–9, emphasis mine). So, actually, it is both presumptuous and inaccurate to refer to *my* faith or *our* faith when, in reality, the faith we have is *God's* faith.

What do we do with it? That's what this book is all about! But in a nutshell, faith must be used. It is active, not passive. It is not a possession, not something to be collected and displayed like stamps or coins, or trophies on a shelf. Faith is energy, a force, an essence.

The Bible says, "For we walk by faith, not by sight" (2 Cor. 5:7). Faith is what empowers us to move, to take action, to accomplish some definite objective or purpose. Faith takes us someplace.

THE FIGHT OF FAITH

VERY EARLY in our existence, we learn that there is a great conflict going on around us. This strife and discord is not found just in the physical world we live in, although violence and contention too often are common elements in our environment. There is also warfare going on in the spirit realm, between the forces of good and evil, between God and the devil. Sooner or later each of us is drawn into this conflict on one side

3

or the other. We cannot stay neutral, so what are we to do when the battle breaks out around us?

The Bible says, "Fight the good fight of faith" (1 Tim. 6:12). In preparation, Paul urges us to "put on the whole armor of God, that ye may be able to stand against the wiles of the devil" (Eph. 6:11). He talks about the belt of truth, the breastplate of righteousness, the helmet of salvation, the sword of the Spirit, and shoes for the preparation of the gospel of peace. "Above all, taking the shield of faith, wherewith ye shall be able to quench all the fiery darts of the wicked" (v. 16).

Our faith is a shield to deflect every fiery dart aimed at us. Faith is our protection against every circumstance that is hatched in hell and against every strategy of Satan. In the words of the great gospel songwriter, Ira Sankey, "Faith is the victory that overcomes the world!"

Spiritual conflict has been going on for centuries, since the fall of Lucifer from heaven. John's Gospel describes one of the battles between the forces of darkness and Jesus, the Word of God, who is the express image of the Father. John wrote, "The light shineth in darkness; and the darkness comprehended it not" (1:5). In English, the word *comprehend* means "to understand," but in Greek the word expresses a far greater scope of meaning. This verse is actually saying that "light" came in the person of Jesus Christ, and "darkness," who is Satan, did everything in his power to put the light out!

4

Now, the devil thought he was successful when Jesus died at Calvary. But Satan really didn't extinguish the light. Jesus said, "No man can *take* my life, but I'll lay it down myself, and in three days I'll pick it up again." (See John 10:17–18.) So the light was hidden for three days and three nights.

But early on Sunday, the first day of the week, the light burst through the darkness, and Jesus rose from the dead!

What does this mean to you and me today? It means that right is stronger than wrong! Truth is stronger than error! Love is stronger than hate! It means that Satan has no power over the family of God, the household of faith. God has given us *Himself*, His Word, His Son. In so doing, He has given us the measure of faith—the God-kind of faith.

And this faith means that we have "power to tread on serpents and scorpions, and over all the power of the enemy: and nothing shall by any means hurt you" (Luke 10:19).

Be sure you understand where this faith comes from. It is not a homemade faith fashioned from truths you try to believe. It is not a body of doctrinal positions that have become a traditional "statement of faith." It is not what looks right, feels good, sounds logical, or seems fair. It is not something magical, mystical, or spooky. Faith is a gift of God, and it is all powerful, unstoppable, and irresistible.

God Wants You to
Use Your Faith

THE ONLY THING that can defeat the faith God has given you . . . is you. You must use your faith, exercise your faith, engage your faith. Until it is pressed into service, faith is only potential. To use the old exercise cliché, you must "use it or lose it!"

Recently I found some grass seed, fertilizer, weed-killer, and other top-quality lawn care products in my garage. I remembered buying those items with my hard-earned money and carrying them home. But I never did anything with them. I meant to. I had big plans and ambitions. Yet, two years after making my resolution, my lawn still looked a bit ragged.

Remember, I had good potential for a fine lawn—a nicely graded lot with good, rich dirt, and concrete edging to mark its boundaries. And I had a good supply of grass seed, a tried-and-proven hybrid strain especially developed for the terrain and weather conditions in my area. I had everything I needed to produce one of the most beautiful lawns on my block. I could even envision my neighbors looking at the lush, green carpet of grass in my yard and saying, "Oh, that looks so nice. It's really beautiful. You did such a good job!"

Except that I never used my seed and lawn care supplies. I never did anything. After two years, I still had all the potential, but my poor yard looked the same.

The supplies were still inside on the garage floor, being tripped over by my family. And my neighbors were thinking, *Why doesn't he do something about that scraggly yard?*

Faith is of no value to anybody unless it is planted. Like seeds, faith must be put in the ground, hidden away, left alone to die and germinate, given the opportunity to produce new life. How many Christians today are walking around, multibillionaires in potential, yet poverty-stricken in their belief and confidence in God?

Your faith should be taking you someplace. Faith activated gets you on the move. But faith is not aimless energy, propelling you in all directions. The psalmist said, "The steps of a good man are ordered by the Lord" (Ps. 37:23). So you ought to be taking God-ordered steps toward a divinely selected destination.

The faith God gave you was intended to be productive. Faith was never supposed to simply sit idle and unused. Nor was it intended to be put on a shelf to be idolized. Faith's purpose always is to be used for the glory of God.

FOLLOW FAITH
WHERE IT LEADS YOU

LET ME remind you that you don't have to produce faith. You don't have to perform great feats to display its talents. Real faith—the God-kind of faith—wants to take you someplace. You simply follow where it leads you. But don't be surprised if the path of faith leads into adverse circumstances, trials, and tribulations. Most of us feel like these are destinations to be avoided. We don't want to go there. And somewhere we got the idea that faith would keep us out of trouble.

What a shock to begin moving in faith, only to find ourselves facing adversity, going into battle, heading straight for trouble. And it soon becomes obvious that instead of being an escape mechanism, faith actually takes us into the fire. In fact, if God is directing us, we're going to have opposition, and there's no way around it. But He will not get us into anything that He cannot get us out of.

Faith does not flee from unpleasant circumstances. Faith does not abandon you and leave you helpless and hopeless because you wake up one morning to find all hell breaking loose right in your house! Faith is not intimidated by pain or suffering, nor does it surrender to fear.

Just the opposite is true. Through faith, God can deliver you. If you are sick, by faith He can heal you. If your family life is all messed up, by faith He can speak peace to the turmoil and bring order out of chaos. You can rest in that. You can have confidence in God. He can open the windows of heaven and pour you out a blessing so amazing and overwhelming that you don't even have room enough to receive it. (See Malachi 3:10.) He can do that. God can send one single angel to straighten out your world and do what you need done in your life by His own sovereign, divine intervention.

But make no mistake—God *is* sovereign. He is not an errand boy, subject to our bidding and manipulation. He works according to His own agenda, on His own timetable, according to His own will.

Understand that the reality of God does not rest on His demonstrated ability to heal heart disease or dissolve malignant tumors. Faith in God is not subject to His opening the eyes of the blind or raising the dead. And contrary to the teachings of the so-called "prosperity gospel," God is not "required" to operate a heavenly commissary that dispenses provisions for all the wants and desires of those who call themselves Christians. God can do all of these things. I believe He does them more often than we even know. But He is still God even if He does *not* do them.

Such a notion is probably shocking to the "high maintenance saints" who make up the membership of the American pop culture religion I call "country-club Christianity." These folks have been conditioned to expect faith to function for their convenience, on their behalf. For them it is a survival tool in the carnal world of houses, cars, jobs, clothing, comfort, and security. They regard themselves as the center of the universe, living for their own personal welfare. They believe that faith repels hardship, brings "stuff" to them, coddles them, entertains them, does everything for them. It takes a lot to please these church members.

This is a sad situation. But don't be too hasty in blaming these spoiled individuals for this state of affairs. They are the product of the American church today. We have produced them; they didn't come like that. The church is in trouble today because it is not spiritually sound. We have gotten away from the basic truths of the gospel and forgotten the fundamentals of God's plan for man. We no longer are concerned about finding and doing God's will, about seeking first the kingdom of God.

Today's church reminds me of the church at Corinth. This was the most talented and gifted church in the New Testament, with strong, foundational teaching, and all the gifts of the Spirit in operation. All the special anointings and callings were present there. Yet the Corinthians were confused people, full of factions and strife, with no sense of direction. It was a worldly church, filled with excesses and abuses. In a letter to the Corinthians, the apostle Paul referred to there being sex sins in the church, with one member even committing the unspeakable—adultery with his father's wife. Paul also dealt with the grievous heresy of church members conducting "Lord's suppers" in which they gorged themselves and got drunk!

How could such a paradox exist? How could these

people who exercised the gifts of the Holy Spirit be caught up in error and outright sin? How could the spiritual gifts reside in people who apparently had no awareness that these gifts were given to strengthen them in faith, to establish them in the Lord, and to glorify Christ Jesus?

The answer is that the manifestation of spiritual power does not carry revelation with it. There is no communication of divine truth, no enlightening disclosure of godly knowledge that accompanies the employment of the gifts of the Spirit. This is why Jesus could heal people before a great crowd of witnesses, and the next week that same multitude could cry out, "Crucify Him!" This is why Jesus could feed a great throng of people on a mountainside, and later tell them, "I am [the] bread of life . . . Except ye eat the flesh of the Son of man, and drink his blood, ye have no life in you" (John 6:48, 53). These same people went away saying He was talking about cannibalism, which the Mosaic law forbade.

REVELATION—
THE RESULT OF OBEDIENT FAITH

REVELATION comes through the Word of God— hearing it, reading it, studying it, praying over it, and allowing the Holy Spirit to guide us into all truth. Revelation is not a one-time experience in which the

11

entirety of the plan of God is dropped into our hearts and minds all at once. It is not captured and encapsulated in a single formula or creed we can memorize and learn once for all time. Revelation is an ongoing, growing experience that unfolds before us as faith takes us down the road of life.

Sometimes God reveals Himself and His truth in very special and dramatic circumstances. While we can and do receive revelation knowledge from the Bible, the written Word, the Lord sometimes moves in an extraordinary way. Some time ago Bishop T. D. Jakes invited me to be a speaker at a large meeting he was conducting in Cincinnati, Ohio. Now, Bishop Jakes is a marvelous preacher, with a large and enthusiastic following of people who enjoy and are blessed by his ministry. So I began working on a special message to preach to the seventeen thousand people who were expected to attend that meeting. I got the inspiration for a message on a great topic, and I could sense that this sermon could be a real blessing to a lot of people. If you're going to speak to that big of a crowd before a man as talented and anointed as Bishop Jakes, it's a good opportunity to show that you can do a little something too.

By the time the meeting began, I felt I was really ready. The night before I was to speak, I went to bed praying and asking God to have His will and use me any way He wanted to. The next morning I woke up weeping, aware that the Spirit of the Lord was moving and dealing with me. The Lord said, "I want you to change your message for this morning. Forget what you have prepared. I want you to preach from Jeremiah where it says, 'I am watching over My word to perform it' (Jer. 1:12; NAS). Tell My people they only need to hear one word from Me."

I prayed and studied that passage from Jeremiah. I didn't have time to develop a sermon outline with the traditional three points and a poem. All I had that morning when I stepped into the pulpit before that great convention crowd was, "You only need to hear one word from God. He will watch over His word and hasten, or hurry, to perform it." All I talked about was the idea of just one word.

But all of a sudden something awesome happened. The presence of the Holy Spirit surrounded me on that platform—above me, before me, behind me, beside me, beneath me. And the anointing of the Holy Ghost poured over me and into me and through me and out of me.

In the process, that one simple scripture, that written Word of God, suddenly became the *rhema*—the spoken Word from the mouth of God Himself! No longer was Andrew Merritt trying to talk—the Lord Almighty, the God of Abraham, Isaac, and Jacob, the Creator of the Universe who spoke the world into existence, He began speaking.

The power of God swept through that auditorium

like a mighty wind. People were weeping, overwhelmed by the awesome presence of God. Some people bowed before Him, some fell down, some lifted their hands in praise. But everybody heard His eloquent proclamation that He had come to fulfill His Word and carry out His promise!

During that amazing visitation of His Spirit, I walked by a lady in a wheelchair and reached out to touch her hand. In an instant she was on her feet, standing, walking, praising God. One word was all she needed to receive her healing. I'll never forget that day when heaven came down and glory filled my soul.

The Bible says, "Faith cometh by hearing, and hearing by the word of God" (Rom. 10:17). A great many Christians think this means listening to a preacher on Sunday morning or playing the latest teaching cassette. But in reality, faith comes when we hear more than the words of a preacher or teacher and tune in the voice of God. Faith comes when the Word brings revelation to our souls.

Where and when does revelation take place in today's church? Why does a majority of today's Christians not know even the basic Sunday school stories or where to locate the various books within the Bible? There is little systematic Bible teaching, book by book, chapter by chapter. Where is the organized emphasis on making the Bible "a lamp unto my feet, and a light unto my path" (Ps. 119:105)?

PRAY THE WILL OF GOD

WHY ARE today's typical Christians novices when it comes to prayer? They know little about the importance of seeking God, crying out to Him, and being nurtured in His presence. They have not been taught to pray, to speak to the Father, to develop a personal, intimate relationship with the Almighty. Many seem uncomfortable or embarrassed about praying in public—or even saying grace at mealtime.

Sadly, the most common form of prayer today is the selfish plea for personal blessings. "Oh, God, I need this. I want that. Give me some of this, that, and the other. Take care of me and my family."

I don't believe God hears that kind of prayer! He does not respond to that kind of request. Jesus said, "Take no thought, saying, What shall we eat? or, What shall we drink? or, Wherewithal shall we be clothed? . . . for your heavenly Father knoweth that ye have need of all these things. But seek ye first the kingdom of God, and his righteousness; and all these things shall be added unto you" (Matt. 6:31–33).

The apostle John declared, "And this is the confidence that we have in him, that, if we ask any thing according to his will, he heareth us" (1 John 5:14).

God knows about us. He knows where we are and what we're going through. And His will for us is good. Philippians 2:13 assures us, "For it is God which worketh in you both to will and to do of his good pleasure."

When the newly liberated nation of Israel was wandering in the wilderness between Egypt and the Promised Land, God gave them manna for food every morning. It might not have been what they wanted, but they had plenty of it. They had a rock that gave them water. They had a cloud for air conditioning in the day and a pillar of flame to provide heat and a nightlight in the darkness. And the Bible says their shoes and clothes never wore out.

God's provisions are always to be found wherever He leads us. So if our faith is taking us someplace—if our faith has us on the move—our needs will be supplied on the go. If we are experiencing real lack, it could well be that we have made a wrong turn, or worse, have simply sat down and are going nowhere. The "things" we need will be found when we get where God has been trying to take us through the leadership of our faith.

The Bible record reveals that throughout history the people who walked close to God and accomplished great things for Him were always people of prayer. From the patriarchs to the prophets, from the first apostles to the great warriors of the faith who carried the gospel to the ends of the earth, the thing God's people all have had in common is the time they spent with Him in prayer. Prayer is the time and place for fellowship, encouragement, comfort, learning, development, and motivation.

Luke's Gospel tells of a prophetess named Anna, who had been a widow for many years. During that time, she "departed not from the temple, but served God with fastings and prayers night and day" (Luke 2:37). She had prayed for God's redemption to be revealed, and recognized the answer to her prayers when Mary and Joseph brought the Christ child to the temple.

The Book of Acts reveals the power that came to the early church through prayer. Peter and John were on their way to the temple at the hour of prayer when they encountered a lame beggar. When asked for a handout, Peter said, "I don't have any silver or gold to give you, but I'll share what I do have! In the name of Jesus Christ of Nazareth, rise up and walk." (See Acts 3:6.) The Bible says, "And he leaping up stood, and walked, and entered with them into the temple, walking, and leaping, and praising God" (v. 8).

All the revivals I know anything about in this country, including the remarkable outpouring of God now taking place in Pensacola, Florida, and in several other American cities, were birthed in prayer. God does absolutely nothing without prayer.

Where is prayer going on today? How many churches even have regular prayer sessions anymore, much less all-day, all-night prayer meetings? The sad truth is that even midweek and Sunday night services have long since been abandoned by a large and growing percentage of today's churches. Sunday morning worship has been neatly streamlined to fit all the church has to offer into a one-hour package. There's twelve minutes of praise and worship, a three-minute musical performance by the choir or a soloist, five minutes for the offering, and another ten minutes for announcements, Bible reading, and maybe a traditional liturgy. Then the minister has twenty minutes or so to do his thing. Add a prayer, a closing hymn, and an invitation for anyone who needs personal ministry, and it's time to go!

Do you ever look at the failures and shortcomings of people and the church and get discouraged? Most of us do from time to time. We shake our heads and wonder if things are ever going to change. Will we ever get it right? Is there no hope for mankind?

Thank God for undying hope and the power of faith. God is not discouraged. He has not given up on you, or me, or on His church. Jesus' disciples once became a little disillusioned and said among themselves, "Who then can be saved? And Jesus looking upon them saith, With men it is impossible, but not with God: for with God all things are possible" (Mark 10:26–27).

We serve the God of the possible. He built the church, and nothing can prevail against it. He can make a way where there seems to be no way. No matter how dark the future may look, He is our light. No matter how many times we have tried and failed, He forgives us, lifts us up, and gives us a fresh start. When

18

all our friends have failed and even our families have forsaken us, He will never leave us.

When life is too much and you're overwhelmed by it all, God is able.

When you think you've lost everything, there's still one thing left. The world didn't give it, and the world can't take it away. It is the secret weapon that will give you victory, the power that will make you an over-comer, the force that is taking you someplace . . . from where you are to where you ought to be. Look inside your heart and you will find it. Reach out to touch it and it will be there.

Faith!

CHAPTER TWO

GOD IS ABLE

NOTHING IS TOO difficult for God. He is the Almighty. The Bible says He "sitteth upon the circle of the earth, and . . . stretcheth out the heavens as a curtain, and spreadeth them out as a tent to dwell in" (Isa. 40:22). He is big. He is strong. I have learned to take the limits off my finite understanding of His ability and power.

One of the most amazing things about God is His interest in mankind, His love for people like you and me, His desire to have fellowship and spend time with us, one on one. The psalmist asked, "What is man, that thou art mindful of him? and the son of man, that thou visitest him?" (Ps. 8:4).

Amazing . . . but true. Jesus said, "For where two or three are gathered together in my name, there am I in the midst of them" (Matt. 18:20). He also promised, "I will never leave thee, nor forsake thee" (Heb. 13:5).

Now, another amazing thing is how much trouble we humans can get ourselves into. We seem to have a natural-born talent for finding difficulty and creating problems. Sometimes it seems that trouble just follows us around, or that the devil has painted a big target on our backs so everybody can shoot at us.

However it happens, people often find themselves in trouble—confused, disappointed, lost, hurting, scared, upset, needy, tired, and discouraged. I can remember many personal experiences when it seemed I spent more time trying to fix things I'd messed up than doing constructive work. I spent more time retracing my steps from wrong turns than traveling in the right direction.

Sometimes I got myself in situations I couldn't correct. At times I fell prey to the devil's deceptions and found myself in desperate straits. I've been in places that looked impossible to get out of. I've had needs so big that there were no visible sources of supply. I've started projects that were so ambitious that they seemed unrealistic—when it appeared that the resources I had to have to succeed were totally unattainable.

Faith in the God of the Impossible

AND IN THOSE difficult times, in the darkest hours, when all hope was gone and disaster seemed unavoidable, God came to my rescue, revealed Himself to me, reached out His strong hand. Time and again He made a way for me when there was no way. He did the impossible. He revealed unexpected solutions. He moved heaven and earth to put the unattainable within my grasp.

Someone might say, "Well, God has blessed you so much because you're a preacher. You are special to Him and not like me." Don't you believe it. God loves everybody the same. He's an equal-opportunity God. What He does for me, He'll do for you. The apostle Peter declared, "God is no respecter of persons" (Acts 10:34).

How does the Lord become the God of the impossible in our lives? Through faith. Jesus said, "If thou canst believe, all things are possible to him that believeth" (Mark 9:23).

God can deliver you—move supernaturally in your life. It doesn't matter what your problem or need may be. Whether your bondage is alcohol or drugs, or you are suffering from cancer or blindness or lameness, there is a God who can stretch forth His hand and break every fetter. He's the God of the impossible!

When doctors say there's no hope, go to God because nothing is too hard for Him. Forget about the religious bumper-sticker rhetoric that says, "When everything else has failed, try God!" No, no, no—don't do that! Pray about everything. Tell God first! Why do you want to go through pain and heartache and live in the misery of a heartbreak hotel? You don't want that! Believe and receive!

You were born to live. You were born to be an eagle instead of a chicken. The mother hen never takes her chicks anywhere but to scratch around in the muck of the barnyard. The mother eagle takes her babies far up into the sky and drops them so they can start flapping their wings and learning to fly! You need to get up and fly! God wants to take you someplace—He's given you faith to carry you out of your barnyard and into the sunlit skies! You were born to soar, to touch the heights.

I've learned to love to live the life of the impossible. The word *impossible* means "the impractical, the inaccessible, the inconceivable, the unfeasible, the insurmountable, the unobtainable." I love that word *unobtainable* because I'm always reaching, always stretching. I'm only satisfied when I'm going for something that is just out of reach. I read in the Bible where it says, "Can two walk together, except they be agreed?" (Amos 3:3). So I don't even hang around or let myself get attached to folks who don't believe anything, don't want anything, and like it exactly where they are.

Don't be afraid of the impossible. Don't be discouraged or disheartened by the unobtainable. Could it be that God gives you a task that makes you stretch, that makes you move? But you won't respond in faith because it looks impossible. So He permits a trial to come. He allows the devil to smack you upside your head. Finally, when you're sick and tired of being sick and tired, you read in the Bible where it says "all things are possible to him that believeth" (Mark 9:23). Or, "with God all things are possible" (Matt. 19:26).

Suddenly faith jumps off the page and arrests you. You begin to see through eyes of faith and to become a person of sight and vision.

God can bring the mountain down. He can fill the valleys and straighten out the crooked way. He can make the rough places smooth and prepare a highway in the wilderness. God can give you favor in the presence of your enemies. He can open doors so that no man can shut them. God is saying, "You can be anything that I design you to be. Put your hand in My hand. Put My Word in your heart. Walk with Me. Talk with Me. Wait upon Me."

The Lord says, "Trust in [Me] with all thine heart; and lean not unto thine own understanding. In all thy ways acknowledge [Me], and [I] shall direct thy paths" (Prov. 3:5–6). "I am the Lord thy God which teachest thee to profit, which leadeth thee by the way that thou shouldest go" (Isa. 48:17).

We are to expect the unexpected . . . the impossible . . . the unattainable. We have to expect God to do something. He is saying, "I'll be whatever you need

Me to be. I'll do whatever you need Me to do."

God knows where you are and what you're going through. He understands the problems you're facing and the dilemma that has you stymied. "There hath no temptation taken you but such as is common to man: but God is faithful, who will not suffer you to be tempted above that ye are able; but will with the temptation also make a way to escape, that ye may be able to bear it" (1 Cor. 10:13).

BIBLE LESSONS ABOUT HOW FAITH WORKS

HAVE YOU ever wondered why the Bible is full of such great stories of every imaginable kind of human experience? There are stories about kings and paupers, men and women, old and young. There are stories of amazing provision, of deliverance, of healing. There are accounts of battles won and victories for single individuals as well as entire nations. There are accounts involving good people and bad, capable, intelligent people and helpless bumblers.

Every story is an example of the power and goodness of God and an object lesson on how faith works.

The Lord knows how to provide for the godly. Matthew's Gospel tells how the tax collector came to Peter to collect the tribute money owed by Jesus and himself. I'm not sure how much they owed, but it seems that tax bills are always too high. And apparently there was not enough money in the disciples' treasury to pay the tax. So Peter brought the problem to Jesus.

The Lord gave Peter some very definite, specific instructions. He said, "I want you to go fishing. Go by yourself—don't take your brother Andrew with you. Don't take your business partners, James and John. This is a job for you alone. When you get down to the shore, don't throw in a net to catch a whole mess of fish. Use a hook so you can catch just one. Take the first fish you catch and look inside its mouth. You'll find a piece of money there that will be enough to pay the taxes due for you and Me." (See Matthew 17:27.)

FOLLOW GOD'S INSTRUCTIONS WITH UNQUESTIONING FAITH

WHEN YOU ASK God to meet a need in your life, be ready to follow God's divine instructions. Notice that in Peter's case his faith took him fishing. Peter might have figured that Jesus would provide the funds to pay the taxes in some other way. He might have expected the Lord to take up an offering from the multitude that came to hear Him teach. And if he had stubbornly waited until Jesus met the need the way he thought it should be done, Peter might still have been waiting. But the Lord had another way to do the job.

When Jesus said, "Go fishing," it would have been natural for Peter to round up his usual fishing buddies.

Sometimes when we're believing God to provide an answer to prayer, we want to get all our friends and prayer partners involved. And every one of them has his own idea about how God should meet our need. If we're not careful, we'll end up trying to use one of our buddy's methods instead of doing what God tells us to do.

God told Peter, "Go. Leave here and get down to the sea. Throw in a hook and catch a single fish. There will be money in its mouth to meet the need." There was a designated *place* to find a designated provision. Don't miss the point here! Your blessing will be found as you obey God's voice and follow His instructions. God's way of meeting your need may be very unexpected. It may come as a strange deliverance. But God doesn't want you looking to the natural for your answers. He wants you to know that He's the God of the supernatural.

One day God told Abraham to take his only son, Isaac, to the land of Moriah and offer him as a sacrifice on one of the mountains there. This was Abraham and Sarah's miracle boy, the son of their old age, the lad they loved dearly. But Abraham got up early the next morning, saddled a donkey, and bundled up the wood he would need for a fire. Then he and Isaac started off for Moriah.

On the third day, the Lord directed Abraham to a specific mountain. He left the donkey and his servants, had Isaac carry the bundle of wood, and brought a container of live coals for the sacrificial fire, and a knife.

As they were climbing up the mountain, Isaac asked his father, "Where is the animal for the sacrifice? We have the wood and the fire, but where is the lamb for the burnt offering?" And Abraham replied, "My son, God Himself will provide a lamb." And they went on up the mountain.

On the mountaintop, Abraham built an altar and spread the wood on the altar. He took his son Isaac, bound him with a rope, and laid him on the altar. Then he took the knife and raised it above his head!

Just then the angel of the Lord spoke and said, "Don't strike your son—for now God knows that you withhold nothing from Him, not even your only son." Abraham then noticed a ram caught by his horns in a thicket, and he offered up the ram as a burnt offering. The Bible says "Abraham called the name of that place *Jehovah-jireh*" (Gen. 22:14)—the Lord my provider.

Did you notice that when Abraham set off on his journey, he didn't know exactly where he was going? God said, "I'll tell you which mountain on the way." Now, what if Abraham had said, "No, I'll just wait right here until You make up Your mind. I like to plan the itinerary for my trip."

Or Abraham well could have argued with God about the purpose of this trip. "You can't be serious about having me sacrifice my son as a burnt offering! This is Isaac, the son You promised me. We had to wait so long for him to be born—his mother was a hundred years old! This is a miracle child. Why would You want me to kill him? I must not be hearing the voice of God about this thing. This doesn't make sense—it can't be right. Let me stay here and pray about this some more until we get it all sorted out."

Or on the way, Abraham could have questioned the choice of mountains. "Why in the world do we need to go way over there? This first mountain looks perfectly fine to me. It even has a trail up the side that would be a much easier climb." Abraham could have climbed the mountain of his choice—the mountain of religion, the mountain of tradition, the mountain of doubt, fear, and unbelief. But if he had climbed the wrong mountain, there would have been no sacrificial ram caught in the bushes!

God has a blessing for you. There is healing, there is deliverance, there is divine intervention for you—but you have to get to the land of Moriah and find the mountain God has chosen. That's where the divine provisions will be!

Matthew's Gospel tells the story of Jesus walking to the disciples on the water. They were out on the Sea of Galilee in a boat that was being tossed and blown by the winds and the waves. The last time the disciples had seen Jesus, He had been going up on a mountain to pray. He had sent them to go on ahead. But when they were in desperate trouble, when their boat was being assailed by the storm, He came to them—

appearing out of the darkness—saying, "Be of good cheer; it is I; be not afraid" (Matt. 14:27).

And Peter, the bold, brash, impetuous disciple who always talked before thinking, who always took action before making a plan, answered Jesus back. He said, "Lord, if it's really You, call me to come to You, walking on the water." (See Matthew 14:28.)

"Come on, Peter," said Jesus. "Walk!"

The Bible says that Peter did it—he walked on the water (v. 29).

Now, most people who tell about this story put most of their emphasis on verse 30, which says that Peter started noticing how strong the winds were blowing, became afraid, and began to sink. Isn't it amazing that people seem to be more interested in Peter's failure than his victory! They read right over verse 29, which says that when Jesus called Peter to come to Him, he got out of the boat and walked on the water. *He did it!*

Yes, Peter did get his eyes off the Master. He did get scared by the crashing waves and howling winds. And he did begin to sink. But the same verse that tells us that also says that he cried out, "Lord, save me."

Immediately Jesus stretched forth His hand and caught Peter. Then the two of them went on together, walking on the water, all the way back to the boat. The way I read the story, Peter walked on the water *twice*, once when Jesus called him to come out of the boat, and the second time when Jesus saved him from sinking and they walked on the water together.

For the record, I'd like to point out that none of the other disciples even got out of the boat! None of them ever walked on the water. Peter is the only man with a testimony of having faith that took him walking on the water. Did Peter fail? Sure—but he got up again. God can always help a man deal with failure. The Bible says, "The steps of a good man are ordered by the Lord: and he delighteth in his way" (Ps. 37:23).

But wait—don't stop. Keep on reading and see what the next verse says! "Though he fall, he shall not be utterly cast down: for the Lord upholdeth him with his hand" (v. 24).

Wow, what a promise! If we fall, God will pick us back up. The man who falls is not a failure. The person who fails to reach his goal on the first try is not a failure. Who is the hopeless case? The person who never tries. He is a failure before he starts!

Be ready to go. Be ready to do. Be ready to try! God will lead you where you need to go. He will help you do what you need to accomplish. He will help you achieve when you take the first step and try. Mark 11:24 says, "What things soever ye desire, when ye pray, believe that ye receive them, and ye shall have them."

REFUSE TO BE DEFEATED

IT'S ALWAYS too soon to quit. You can never be defeated

until you quit trying. When God is involved, just when it appears that all hope is gone, the unexpected happens. The impossible takes place.

I love the Bible story about a woman who had suffered from a very serious hemorrhaging condition—the Bible calls it "an issue of blood"—for twelve long years. She had suffered many things of physicians, spent all the money she had, and had gotten worse instead of better. Has that ever happened to you? Have you ever gone to the specialists, had all the treatments, bought all the expensive medicine, and even gone through painful surgery, and ended up in worse shape than when you started?

Well, then you need to pay close attention to this Bible account. The woman with the issue of blood did not seem to know when she was defeated—when it was all over—when it was time to give up. She had suffered pain, misery, and rejection. But she just kept on going.

One day when things had gotten as bad as they could get, she heard about Jesus. Someone told her about this man "who went about doing good, and healing all that were oppressed of the devil" (Acts 10:38). She heard that He was the God of the impossible who helped people obtain the unobtainable. She heard about the miracles Jesus performed, the people who were delivered, the lame who walked, the deaf whose ears were unstopped, the blind who saw. She heard these things, and her faith rose up within her. And this poor woman said, "I'm going to find this Jesus. If He's helping others, He can help me. If I can just touch the hem of His garment, I know I will be made whole."

Faith is in your heart. The Bible says, "Out of the abundance of the heart the mouth speaketh" (Matt. 12:34). Your words express what is in your heart. And your heart is filled with positive things like "I can" and "I will." When you hear words like "I can't," you're reading the wrong script. That comes from the mind, not the heart. The mind thinks it is the writer and producer of your life, but it isn't. The heart is! The script should not say, "I can't" but "He can!"

The woman with the issue of blood got up and did something about what she heard. She set out to obtain the unobtainable—by touching the hem of Jesus' garment. She knew the answer she needed was in Him. She understood what David meant when he said, "I will lift up mine eyes unto the hills, from whence cometh my help. My help cometh from the Lord" (Ps. 121:1–2).

According to the Old Testament law, the woman was ceremoniously unclean because of her issue of blood. She was supposed to be quarantined from the rest of the people. She was subject to certain rituals of cleansing before she could be out in society again. For her to be in the midst of people—especially men—was culturally unacceptable. But she said, "I'm going to go find Jesus. I'm tired of suffering. I'm tired of being excluded from society. I'm tired of being in pain, misery, and rejection."

So she plunged into the crowd and pushed her way through the press of people. She said, "I have to be in His presence—I have to touch Him."

Faith is determined. Faith is persistent. Faith has a destination. Faith makes its way through the throngs, reaches out and touches the hem of Jesus' garment. So when that little woman got close to Jesus and reached out, it wasn't her fingers that touched Him—it was her faith! At that instant, something happened to Jesus. He turned around and said, "Who touched Me?" He recognized that virtue had gone out of His body. Somebody had put a demand on the anointing. Somebody's touch had faith in it.

They found the woman and brought her, trembling, into Jesus' presence, face to face. She told her story— why she had to touch the hem of His garment. And when she had explained, He said, "Woman, thy faith has made thee whole!"

Now, the story relates that the woman had suffered many things of doctors, and had spent all the money she had. No doubt the doctors had been giving her bad reports. No doubt they'd said, "You're never going to be well. Nothing can cure you. Your case is hopeless."

I'm telling you—don't listen to bad reports. Stop listening to the discouraging words of the doomsday brigade. They will tell you that you're never going to get blessed. "You're always going to live in poverty," they say. "You'll always have a low-paying job. Your marriage will never work. Your home is out of order. Your kids won't obey you. Nothing works for you. You go to church and nothing happens. Things don't look good!"

Don't listen to negative reports. The Word says, "Be still, and know that I am God" (Ps. 46:10). God can do the impossible. He has no limits. He cannot be defeated. He is able!

Now, when that woman saw the crowds around Jesus, she was not discouraged. They couldn't help her, and they couldn't stop her from being blessed. The woman said, "It's not what you know—it's what I know. It's not what you want—it's what I want." So she pressed on. And it was a struggle.

Getting what you need from God may involve a struggle. Seldom will the answer to your need just drop into your lap out of the sky! But when you begin acting on your faith, moving out into the flow of the Spirit, God will also take action and move toward you. When you do all you can do, you can expect God to do all He can do. And that's always enough to bring deliverance and victory. The Bible says, "The eyes of the Lord run to and fro throughout the whole earth, to show himself strong in the behalf of them whose heart is perfect toward him" (2 Chron. 16:9).

Are you ready to receive from God? You don't need any more information. You have a faith tape library. You have books in your bedroom, tapes in your car, and tapes to go to sleep by. You have more knowledge and information already than you know what to do with. It's time to put some of it to work—to start walking with Jesus, to start letting your faith take you someplace where you've never been before.

MOSES AND EXODUS

ONE OF THE greatest deliverance stories in all of the Bible is the story of the children of Israel being led out of the slave camps of Egypt where they had been imprisoned for four hundred years. It is a perfect example of the unlimited power of faith on the move, going someplace!

The Israelites were in an impossible situation—hopeless, end of the line, no win. What they saw with their natural eye filled their hearts with terror and despair. But God moved by His own divine intervention on their behalf. And what He did for them was not a temporary, stop-gap measure. It was not a Band-Aid, two-aspirin fix. The salvation and deliverance God prepared for them was for today and forever. When God takes care of a problem, it's fixed right.

Don't be afraid of your problem. God does not want you to be motivated and controlled by fear. He will come to dispel and rebuke your fears. "For God hath not given us the spirit of fear; but of power, and of love, and of a sound mind" (2 Tim. 1:7). If the spirit of fear didn't come from God, it must have come from the devil. He is the source of doubt, fear, and torment.

God gives us just the opposite. He gives us power, love, and a sane, sound mind—He gives us faith. The God-kind of faith will capture and conquer every fear. With faith, you can look square in the face of life's circumstances and tell your fears to get lost. The God of the impossible has authorized you to notify fear to leave you alone. You don't have to hide from trouble. You don't have to run from problems. Instead, in every situation, in all your ways, seek the Lord, acknowledge Him, and let Him direct your path.

You don't need to seek healing—seek the Healer. You don't need to seek salvation—seek the Lord of salvation. You don't need to seek deliverance—seek the Deliverer. "But seek ye first the kingdom of God, and his righteousness; and all these things shall be added unto you" (Matt. 6:33).

God had prepared a man to be His representative, His instrument, to lead His chosen people out of Egypt. His name was Moses. Now, Moses was a little rough around the edges. He didn't much look like a deliverer. And he didn't much act like a champion, ready to overcome. When the time came for Israel's prayers to be answered, Moses was on the back side of the desert, sitting on the dark side of a mountain. He had been out there herding sheep for forty years.

One day Moses was shuffling along in the desert when he saw a strange sight—a bush that was on fire, but not consumed by the fire. He turned aside to go see this strange phenomenon. And when he turned, God saw Moses and spoke to him. He said, "Take off your shoes, for you are standing on holy ground." In other words, "The bush might be over yonder, but I'm here. The fire in the bush is an attraction—and it is My doing . . . it is a part of Me. But I'm over here too."

The God of the impossible is not in just the obvious supernatural, but He is also right on your path in the midst of the desert experience. He is right where you are. If you are in a mess, He's right there in your mess. Wherever you are, God is. If you're on the mountain, He's on the mountain. And if you're in the valley, He's in the valley. Wherever you are, God is. He is always near to His beloved.

God had a reason for telling Moses to take off his shoes. In the culture of that day, only free men wore shoes. God was telling Moses, "If you're going to be My man, you can't be free—you have to be a slave! I want you to be My servant. Take off your shoes, for the ground you're standing on is holy ground." And when Moses instantly obeyed, God said, "All right, I have a job for you. There are some descendants of Abraham, Isaac, and Jacob who are in slavery down in Egypt. I have heard their cries, and it is time for them to go free. I want you to go see the Pharaoh."

God heard the prayers of the children of Israel down in the slave camps of Egypt. They didn't know He heard them. They thought they had been forgotten and abandoned. There was no sign that God even knew they existed. But when they cried out, beseeching Him with tears and anguish of heart, He heard them and started working on their behalf.

While they were crying, the God of the impossible was doing something behind the scenes. While their tears were flowing, He was preparing their deliverance. While they were crying, He was making a way where there seemed to be no way. While they were crying, God was preparing a messenger to bring them a word from God.

"Go deliver my people from Egypt," God said. But Moses responded, "Wait a minute. I know something about this Pharaoh. I've lived in his house, and was adopted by his daughter. Egypt is a wicked, evil nation, with a multiplicity of gods. Pharaoh will not be impressed with a vagabond from the desert wandering in to tell him to give up his free labor force. If I go, I need to know that You're with me."

So God said, "Throw your rod down on the ground." When Moses obeyed, his rod became a serpent, wriggling on the sand. God said, "Pick it up again—by the tail." Now, I don't know a lot about snakes, but I do know that if you're going to pick one up, you take hold of it just behind its head so it can't turn and bite you. But God said, "Pick it up by the tail." And as soon as Moses touched that serpent by the tail to pick it up, it became a rod again.

God was showing something meaningful to Moses.

40

The Egyptian Pharaohs wore an emblem on their head-piece that was in the form of a serpent. God was showing Moses that he could come to grips with Pharaoh and overpower him—that he could pick up the serpent by the tail and destroy it with the help of God.

Moses required a lot more convincing. But God patiently prepared Moses for his mission, equipping him to do the job he had been called to do. The Book of Exodus is fascinating reading, with a clear but amazing narrative of the God of the impossible at work. Every believer should read it often as a reminder of the lengths to which the Lord will go to answer the prayers of His people.

When Moses went into the palace of the ruler of Egypt, the Pharaoh was not greatly impressed. He refused to take seriously Moses' demand that he let the people of Israel go free. Instead, he increased the misery of the people. "If the people are wanting to go out into the wilderness to worship God, as you say, they must have too much time on their hands," said Pharaoh. "We'll stop providing them with straw to use in making bricks. They can use the extra time they have to gather their own straw—and they still must produce the same amount of bricks."

Then Moses started delivering God's ultimatums to Pharaoh. "If you don't let the people go, the water in the rivers will be turned to blood."

Pharaoh would resist every ultimatum, then when

the threat was carried out, he would say, "Okay, I'll give in. The Israelites can go free." But he wouldn't keep his word. And there would be a new ultimatum! Ten times this happened.

The last ultimatum was the unthinkable. "If you don't let God's people go, God will smite dead the first-born son of every household." But despite all the plagues that had befallen the Egyptians, Pharaoh still refused to give in.

On the last night, God said, "This is the *exodus*—the 'coming out.' Tell the people to get a lamb for every household, kill it, and apply its blood upon the mantel and doorpost. Tonight when the death angel moves across the land of Egypt, when he sees the blood, he will pass over your houses. But the houses of the Egyptians will not be spared."

The next morning there was an unending shriek of horror and grief from one side of Egypt to the other. The oldest sons of every Egyptian family were dead! The death angel had even visited the Pharaoh's house! But the houses of Israel with blood on the doorposts were spared. And finally the Pharaoh was ready to send the Israelites on their way out of Egypt.

FAITH IN THE BLOOD OF JESUS

THE STORY of the passover in Egypt is a *type* or shadow, a foretelling of the saving blood of Jesus Christ. While lambs provided the blood to go on the doorposts of the Israelites, Jesus became the sacrificial Lamb to provide the precious blood that washes away the sins of the world from the heart of each individual who comes to Him.

If you're going to understand how to deal with the God of the impossible, you must know about the power of the blood of Christ. When Adam sinned, God sacrificed a lamb on his behalf. He took the wool and the skin of the animal to make a covering garment for him, and He took the blood to atone for and cover Adam's sin. And from that time on, starting with Adam's son Abel, man offered the blood of sacrificial animals as an offering for the sins of himself and his household. Later, with the institution of the priesthood, the descendants of Aaron went into the holy of holies in the temple on the day of atonement, and sprinkled blood on the mercy seat to seek forgiveness of sins for all the people in the nation. But there could be no substitute for the sacrifice of the blood.

Then, forty-two generations after Adam's day, Jesus Himself came to the world as the Lamb of God, slain from the creation of the world, and shed His blood at Calvary for the sins of the world. Once and for all, the divine blood of Jesus was poured out on the mercy seat of eternity, "that whosoever believeth in him should not perish, but have everlasting life" (John 3:16).

The sentence of death still hangs over the world as a penalty for sin. But God says, "If you accept my Son,

Jesus, though your sins be as scarlet, they shall be as white as snow." (See Isaiah 1:18.) "And when I see the blood of Christ covering the guilt-stained parts of your life, I will pass over you."

Sadly, much of the modern church doesn't want to have anything to do with the blood. They have all kinds of rituals and programs, they teach all kinds of information. But people don't learn about the blood of Jesus. So many of today's Christians don't understand the necessity of the blood, or the power of the blood. And without the blood, you can have no relationship with the God of the impossible.

When God led Israel out of Egypt, His presence was signified by a great pillar that was visible to all that great company—at least three million people (and maybe twice that many). The pillar was a cloud by day and a fire by night. When the pillar moved, the people were to march with it. When the pillar stopped, the people were to stop. As long as they stayed under the pillar, they were safe.

Josephus, the Jewish historian, said that God could have taken Israel into Canaan in two or three days if He had led them on a direct path. But He did not take them on the normal route. Why? Because it would have taken them through the land of the Philistines, who were people of war. The Israelites had been slaves to the Egyptians for four hundred years. They had developed a slave mentality. They were accustomed to having their food provided, their clothes provided, and their day planned for them. Someone had always told them where to go and what to do, so they had developed a docile, non-resisting slave mentality. If this great assembly of people had been placed in a hostile military situation, they would have been easy pickings for any army. Because they weren't used to fighting, they would have become fearful during any conflict and would have helped destroy themselves.

So God moved the camp into safe territory. And, in the beginning, He did not move them out of Egypt. They had been led out of bondage—out of slavery—but not out of Egypt.

After a while, when the funerals were over for the dead sons of Egypt, Pharaoh once again rebelled against God. Although he had freed the Israelites and told them they could go, after a little time went by, Pharaoh wanted to get them back. Understand this, my friend. The devil wants to take you back. Egypt is a type of the world. The world wants you back. The devil doesn't want to turn you loose and let you go. The devil wants to capture you again and try to reclaim your allegiance to him. But there is a struggle involved! The God of the impossible will not stand idly by and allow the devil to do that unopposed.

When Pharaoh discovered that the people of Israel were still camped in Egypt, he decided to send his army after them and bring them back into captivity to work as his slaves. Never mind that he had given his word to let them go after a long series of negotiations. Never mind that every time he'd broken his word to Moses before, the nation of Egypt had suffered grievous plagues. Never mind that his rebellious nature had directly caused the death of all the firstborn sons in every family in the nation. Pharaoh had in mind to bring the Israelites back to the slave camps and take out his frustration, grief, and anger on them.

So he ordered all his military troops to gather for pursuit and battle. He brought together all his horses and chariots. He had a meeting with his generals and said, "Go after the Israelites and capture them. Bring Moses and all the people back here to me. Don't come back without them!"

Strategically, the people of Israel were located in a very bad situation. On one side of their camp were badlands—rugged hills and terrain too rough for a great company of people to pass through. On the other side, a few miles away, was an Egyptian garrison where Pharaoh's border patrol was stationed. These were the troops that normally would have protected the coast area from any infiltration or attack. In front of the Israelites lay the Red Sea. Now, some scholars have said the Red Sea wasn't a really great body of water—that it was never very deep, and that at some times of the year it dried up until it was little more than a creek or a pond. I don't know about that. All I can be sure of is that on this occasion, the Red Sea was big enough and deep enough to be an uncrossable barrier for three to six million people!

Oh, one last thing—behind the Israelites, coming up fast, was Pharaoh's army.

Moses and the children of Israel were in an impossible situation. And the Israelites were fearful and panicky. When they looked back and saw the dust clouds in the distance from the Egyptian army closing in, they said, "Old Pharaoh is never going to let us go. He just won't give up. We're in for big trouble now!"

Turning to Moses, they said, "You should have just left us alone. Why did you want to bring us out here to die?"

Then they started telling lies and having "selective" memory. "We were doing fine before you came and disturbed us," they cried. "At least there were no graves in Egypt!"

They knew that wasn't true! They forgot about the hard taskmasters who demanded more and more work from them. They forgot about the beatings, the scourgings, the daily humiliations. Four hundred years of slavery had warped their mentality.

And they said to Moses, "You should have left us back there."

That's when Moses said to the people, "Fear ye not, stand still, and see the salvation of the Lord, which he will show to you today: for the Egyptians whom ye have seen today, ye shall see them again no more for ever. The Lord shall fight for you, and ye shall hold your peace" (Exod. 14:13–14).

Faith Always Moves Forward

Then Moses commanded the Israelites to get ready to march. "Go forward!" he commanded. The path of faith is always forward. Faith never backs up. Faith never turns around. Faith always proceeds straight ahead, onward, forward! The people up front must have wondered why Moses was preparing to march them straight into the sea. But Moses had been in communication with the God of the impossible. He knew what was going to happen.

God instructed Moses to stretch forth his rod over the sea and command the waters to roll back. And that's what he did. Now, I don't know exactly how it happened. The Bible says a wind blew the waters back—it had to be a supernatural wind from the God who is able to do the impossible.

At the same time, the angel of the Lord caused a cloud to hide the people from the Egyptian army coming up behind them. And the Israelites walked across the Red Sea on dry land. As the Israelites were arriving on the other side, the army of Pharaoh went rushing into the path across the sea. The cloud lifted so Moses and the Israelites could see what was about to happen! In the middle of the sea, the wheels of the chariots began to bog down and fall off. In no time at all, there was a terrible traffic jam right in the middle of the sea—horses running on top of fallen soldiers, with shouts, screams, and curses filling the air as the troops tried to keep on moving their weapons and equipment across the sea. Then, when Pharaoh's armies were all the way inside the watery walls with no way to get back, the wind stopped blowing.

The walls of water started collapsing, and the path through the sea disappeared. There was a boiling and churning of mud and blood as the sea swallowed up the Egyptians in a mighty crashing roar—and the choppy waves rolled away until the surface of the sea once again was calm and still. Except for some debris scattered on the surface, and a floating lump here and there, little could be seen. The mighty pursuing army had totally disappeared.

The Egyptians could not be seen! Not then . . . not ever again.

The word of the Lord proved itself to be true. As the Israelites obeyed the command to stand still, without fear, they did, indeed, see the salvation of the Lord. The word translated "Lord" in Exodus 14:13 is the Hebrew word, *El Shaddai,* which means "the Almighty, the God who is stronger than any god, the God of all power, the God of more than enough." And there's one more meaning, according to the Andrew Merritt translation—"the God of the impossible."

It may be that the circumstances of your life have pushed you into a corner. You may feel that—like the Israelites—you're trapped between the devil and the deep blue sea. You can't go to the right. You can't go to the left. And you can't go back. There's only one way to go, and from a human standpoint, it looks unlikely, improbable, unrealistic, impossible!

Well, you may well be approaching holy ground, the place where miracles happen. But don't stop here. Go forward. You must keep moving. Even if it appears that you are marching into the sea, remember that *El Shaddai* is your Lord, the God of the unattainable, the God of the impossible. He is the God who can do for you what you cannot do for yourself. He is able! Nothing is too hard or too difficult for Him.

Don't stay locked in to your past. Don't keep focusing on yesterday with its heartaches and problems. It's not important how many people have disappointed you, failed you, and done you wrong. The crucial issue now is not what they did, but what God has done . . . and what He's going to do. Go forward. Keep believing. Keep moving! March on toward the impossible.

The Bible says, "This one thing I do, forgetting those things which are behind, and reaching forth unto those things which are before, I press toward the mark for the prize of the high calling of God in Christ Jesus" (Phil. 3:13–14).

CHAPTER THREE

GOD IS WILLING

SOMETIMES WE HEAR about God doing wonderful things for people in Bible times, and we are amazed. We believe that God did those things, but it is astonishing to us. We can barely believe the miraculous power that God used for the welfare of people in Bible times. We believe that God *could* do such things—that He is able—but we find it much more difficult to comprehend that God is willing to do such things for *anyone* who can believe . . . and that He still will do them today. The Bible says, "Jesus Christ the same yesterday, and today, and for ever" (Heb. 13:8), and "All things are possible to him that believeth" (Mark 9:23).

We need to have an intimate relationship with God so we can see Him as He really is. Only through having a personal relationship with the Lord can we grasp the idea that God's miracle power is available to us—that the impossible can happen to *us,* not somebody else.

Christ is in the midst of His church. Jesus said, "If two of you shall agree on earth as touching any thing that they shall ask, it shall be done for them of my Father which is in heaven. For where two or three are gathered together in my name, there am I in the midst of them" (Matt.18:19–20). "Be strong in the Lord, and in the power of his might" (Eph. 6:10).

When I read the Bible, I try to read it as though my Father, who loves me, is writing to me. He wants me to know His divine character. And so He uses parables, examples, and stories about various real people to help me understand how much He loves us. One of my favorite Bible stories is found in Matthew 8.

"When he [Jesus] was come down from the mountain, great multitudes followed him. And, behold, there came a leper and worshiped him, saying, Lord, if thou wilt, thou canst make me clean. And Jesus put forth his hand, and touched him, saying, I will; be thou clean. And immediately his leprosy was cleansed. And Jesus saith unto him, See thou tell no man; but go thy way, show thyself to the priest, and offer the gift that Moses commandeth, for a testimony unto them" (Matt. 8:1–4).

In Bible times, there was a specific way infectious diseases like leprosy were to be dealt with. First of all, the priest determined who was clean or unclean depending on the kind of blemish or sore an individual might have. If the priest saw that it was a wound that would not heal or was spreading and getting worse, he proclaimed the sufferer unclean, a leper. Then he took steps to protect other people from possible infection, to prevent an epidemic of the disease.

Lepers were quarantined from society, not allowed to live inside the city walls and associate with other people. Usually they lived in colonies with other lepers, isolated from families and friends. Not only were they kept away, they were required to identify themselves if anyone came near them. They were to cry out, "Unclean, unclean!" so other people would know to avoid any contact with them.

Failure to observe these rules was a serious offense. The penalty could be death.

The Bible says that when Jesus came down from the mountain where He had gone to pray, a great multitude followed him. According to the law, any leper who saw such a crowd was to identify himself and move out of the way. But the story of the leper who came to Jesus in Matthew 8 shows a man who was desperate and was literally risking *everything*—even his life—to come to the Lord. This leper came into the multitude, made his way to where Jesus was, and worshiped Him.

What was this man doing in the midst of the crowd when he had been condemned to the leper colony? What gave him the audacity to leave his confinement and seek out Jesus when the priest had declared him unclean?

Reckless Faith

People often don't understand faith. Faith is reckless. Faith does not always obey man's rules. Faith does not resign itself to whatever conditions or circumstances may come. Faith looks at leprosy and says, "You can't destroy me . . . you can't get me down. All I need to do is get to Jesus. If I can get to Jesus, He can change my circumstances."

We are involved with a supernatural God who says, "Is any thing too hard for [Me]?" (Gen. 18:14). Our God is able and willing to save, heal, and deliver, and to set the captive free. When the anointing of the Holy Ghost comes, people get healed, delivered, and set free by the power of the living God.

Why is it that some people can get healed in a miracle service and other people sitting there don't feel a thing? When a crowd gathers, most of them don't get anything—they don't even know what's going on. But a few are making contact with the transforming, life-changing power of God. And on this particular day with Jesus, the multitude was just walking along, and all of a sudden, here came this unclean man, this leper who had broken out of the sanitarium and made his way to Jesus.

It wasn't easy for this man to get to Jesus. He had to get out of the leper colony. He had to get away from those who wanted to discourage him. He had to drag his sick, weak body over the rough terrain outside the city. And when he got to the edge of the multitude gathered around Jesus, he had to start making his way through the crowd. He had to push a little, squeeze through some tight spots, and keep on moving ahead.

When you start to get closer to the Lord, there will be some folks you'll have to walk over to get to Him. There will be some circumstances you'll have to push through to get into His presence. There may be some things you'll have to push out of the way or go around to get the Lord.

When the leper got inside the press of the crowd and came into the presence of the Lord, he fell down and worshiped Him. He began to praise God and acknowledge His worthiness. He recognized Jesus as the mighty God, the King of kings and the Lord of lords.

When the man with leprosy worshiped Jesus, he got His attention! Jesus was ministering to a whole multitude of people. They were just standing around, crowding in close to Him, and He was teaching them as they walked along. But when this leper broke through and began to worship Him, Jesus focused

His attention on that man.

The leper said, "Lord, if thou wilt, thou canst make me clean." He didn't say, "If You're able, do something for me. If You have the power, help me out." He recognized and acknowledged the power of Jesus. In effect, he was saying, "Now, Lord, I already *know* You can."

Is it God's will to heal the sick? Here was the perfect test case. This would set the precedent for all the cases that came after. Here was the opportunity for Jesus to say, "I only heal certain people who have the right social standing. I only heal the easy cases. It's really My will for some people to suffer. So why don't you get out of here and go back to the leper colony!"

But Jesus didn't say that. He didn't even stop and think about the situation before He made up His mind. The Bible says that Jesus put forth His hand and *touched* the leper. He touched the unclean man! And He said, "I will, be thou clean." And *immediately* the leprosy was cleansed. (See Matthew 8:1–3.) The man was made whole. He was set free. And Jesus declared, for everybody, for all time, "It is My will that you be healed!"

This man had been an unwanted leper, an outcast of society, a man condemned by the law of Moses, with no hope, no help, no future. But he was arrested by faith and brought into the presence of Jesus. And the Lord, anointed by the Holy Ghost and power, reached forth His hand and touched him. In order for Jesus to remain the Lamb of God, without spot or blemish, He had to heal the leper. Otherwise, He would have been contaminated by the disease and would not have been perfect and clean.

Jesus wants to heal you. It is His will that you be healed and delivered and set free. In spite of your situation, no matter how big a mess you've made of your life, no matter how contaminated you are by sin and disease, God will step in the midst of it and will touch you. And when He touches you, "Old things are passed away . . . all things are become new" (2 Cor. 5:17). You are healed and whole, forgiven and restored.

Many people seem to have a hard time understanding that it is God's will to meet their needs and help them be successful and victorious in life. Like the leper, they are sure He *could* do it if He wanted to, but they are not so sure He is willing to. So their prayers turn into begging, pleading, and bargaining sessions. They pray as if they are trying to get God's attention and overcome His reluctance to bless them. They wheedle and cajole, plead and promise. And all their efforts are as useless as trying to unlock an open door!

Indeed, Jesus said, in effect, "Not only am I willing, but I'm eager to minister to you." What is God's attitude toward us? Revelation 3:20 records these words: "Behold, I stand at the door, and knock: if any man hear my voice, and open the door, I will come in to him, and will sup with him, and he with me."

Because It's God's Will, It Shall Be Well

I LOVE THE Old Testament story of the Shunammite woman. It is a classic example of the will of God for His people—to reward them for faithful service and to be available in time of need.

Second Kings tells the story of the prophet Elisha traveling to the small town of Shunem during his ministry travels. The Bible says there was "a great woman" there, and she invited him to come to her house to eat. The woman and her husband became great friends to the prophet, and every time he passed through Shunem, he stopped by their house to eat and spend the night.

In fact, he came so often that the woman said to her husband, "Let's build a room on to the house for Elisha, and put in a bed, a table, a stool, and a candlestick, so he'll have everything he needs whenever he comes this way." (See 2 Kings 4:10.) "Elisha is a holy man of God. This is a way we can help him and have a part in what he is doing for the kingdom of God."

The next time Elisha came to their house, he had his own room . . . and his own key to the door. After supper, Elisha went into his new room and tried out the bed. Can't you imagine how nice it must have seemed to the man of God to have a comfortable place to rest and pray, sheltered from the open road and secure from the dangers of robbers and highwaymen?

Elisha had his servant call the Shunammite woman and express his appreciation for her care. "See if there is some favor I can do for her. I have good political connections with the king and the commander of the local army post—shall I put in a good word for her?"

The woman told the servant, "Thanks, but no thanks. I dwell among my own people, and we take care of ourselves. We don't need anything."

When the servant relayed the woman's reply to Elisha, he said, "There must be something she needs that we could do."

The servant said, "The only thing I can think of is that she and her husband have no children, and her husband is an old man."

"That's it," said Elisha. "Tell her to come in here." And when the woman came to see what he wanted, the prophet said, "You have blessed me, and I want to express my appreciation. So here's what is going to happen—about this time next year, you will be holding a baby in your arms—your own son." (See 2 Kings 4:12–16.)

The woman was overcome. Having a son was tremendously important to families in the culture of that day. A son received the inheritance of his family and carried on the family name. Having a son was considered a mark of prosperity and blessing. Being totally childless was considered to be a curse.

"Don't tell me something like this if it isn't true!" the woman said. "This is more than I could possibly hope for. Certainly I did not minister to you in hopes of receiving anything in return."

Of course, the words of the man of God were fulfilled and came true. The woman conceived and gave birth to a child, a son (v. 17). What a time of rejoicing and celebration must have gone on when that little boy was born. And don't you know he was the joy of their lives. I can imagine that when Elisha came to stay in his room at the house, he must have taken delight in seeing this child growing into a fine son, being raised in the nurture and the admonition of the Lord.

You can read this whole story for yourself in the fourth chapter of 2 Kings. It's an amazing story of faith.

One day when the little boy had grown big enough to have some chores to do and could do a few things to help, he went out into the fields with his father, where the reapers were harvesting grain. And after a while, the boy said to his father, "My head hurts. My head hurts so bad!" So the father had one of his servants pick up the lad and carry him back to the house to his mother. She washed his face with a cool cloth and held him gently in her lap, doing all she knew to do for him. But about noon the boy died.

Put yourself in the place of this woman. After giving up hope that you'd ever have a child, the man of God tells you that you're going to give birth to a son to present to your husband. "Don't joke about this!" you say. "Don't tell me this is going to happen unless it's true. I couldn't stand to get my hopes up and then be bitterly disappointed." But the miracle does happen, and the child of your husband's old age is born. Then, just as he has become the center of your world and the pride of your life, in an instant this precious son is cruelly snatched away! How would you feel? What would you do?

Would you shriek and moan in the throes of grief and despair? Would you be angry at the prophet you'd done so much for? Would you be bitter toward the God who would torment you so?

That's not what the Shunammite woman did. She calmly got up and carried the lifeless body of her one and only son, the pride of her life, and laid him upon the bed in the room her husband had built for Elisha the prophet. Then she came out and shut the door.

She went out to talk to her husband. "Get one of the servants to saddle a donkey, and come go with me. I'm going to find the man of God; then I'll be back." She didn't even tell him that their child was dead.

The father must have sensed that something unusual was going on. "Why are you going to see Elisha?" he said. "It's not the Sabbath or a special holiday worship season."

"I'm going!" she said. "It shall be well!"

Can you see it? No tears, no despair, no harsh criticism of Elisha, no bitter denunciation of God and His Word. She had lived her whole life trying to be a blessing, trying to do the right thing. Now her reward and blessing had become a great trial and torment. The thing she held most precious in the world had just been snatched from her hands.

"My son was born late in my life by the will of God! I did not seek it or ask for it. In fact, I told the prophet not to even mention such a thing to me if it was not to be true. But the baby came! And he became a fine little boy, the most precious thing in the world to my husband and me. God gave us this wonderful blessing. It was His will. 'Every good gift and every perfect gift is from above, and cometh down from the Father of lights, with whom is no variableness, neither shadow of turning' (James 1:17). '[The Lord's] compassions fail not. They are new every morning: great is [His] faithfulness. The Lord is my portion, saith my soul; therefore will I hope in him. The Lord is good unto them that wait for him, to the soul that seeketh him' (Lam. 3:22–24). Therefore, I cannot believe God would destroy me and desert me now. So I will not despair. I will go to God's prophet. And it shall be well!"

Get the message here. Don't miss it! When you know you are living in God's will, you can also know that *it shall be well* in everything that touches your life.

- Let sickness and disease afflict you. *It shall be well.*
- Let opposition and difficulty cross your path.
  It shall be well.
- Let darkness and disappointment come near.
  It shall be well.
- Let sorrow and loss bring you to your knees.
  It shall be well.
- Nothing the devil can do will defeat you.
  God is greater than he is, and He will never
  leave you nor forsake you. *It shall be well!*

The woman got on the donkey and told the servant, "Head for Mount Carmel where Elisha is. Don't stop for anything and don't slow down until I tell you." And they hurried down the dusty road—hour after hour, mile after mile—going to find the man of God.

When they got close to where Elisha was, he looked up and saw her coming. He said to the servant, "Run now . . . to meet her, and say to her, Is it well with thee? is it well with thy husband? Is it well with the child?" (2 Kings 4:25–26).

The woman certainly realized that she was in the middle of the crisis of her life. Her only son had died in her arms. Her husband was at home, old and weary, bewildered and confused by what was going on. And upstairs, in the prophet's chamber lay the cold, still body of her precious little boy. How would you have felt? How would you have answered when the servant of the man of God asked, "Are you okay? Is your husband okay? Is your child okay?"

The woman answered Elisha's servant, "It is well!" She kept right on going toward the man of God. She didn't stop or slow down until she came into his presence.

Falling down to the ground before Elisha, she grabbed hold of his feet. The servant of the prophet tried to pull her away, but she held on. Elisha said, "Let her alone" (v. 27).

When you try to claim the promises of God and hold on for the victory, there's always someone who tries to discourage you. Don't turn loose! Don't let anybody stop you or talk you out of holding onto what God wants you to have. When people say, "Just accept the loss and admit defeat," don't give up. Hold on and keep saying, "It is well!"

The woman reminded Elisha that she hadn't asked God for a child against His will. "In fact," she said, "I told you, 'Don't tell me I'll have a baby if it is not to be.'"

Elisha told his servant, "Take my staff and run back to her house. Don't stop even to speak to anybody on the road. Get there as fast as you can, and lay my staff upon the body of her child." (See 2 Kings 4:28–29.) The servant took off as fast as he could go.

Now, the woman could have said, "Well, this is all I could ask. If Elisha's staff doesn't restore my son, I'll just have to accept his death and get ready to bury him. At least I tried." But that's not what she did. She said,

"As the Lord lives, and as your soul lives, I won't leave you. There's only one answer I'll accept."

So Elisha got up and went with her on the road back to her house. After a long while, his servant came back to meet him. "I laid your staff on the boy, but nothing happened," he reported.

When they got back to Shunem, Elisha went up to his chamber where the dead body of the child was laying on his bed. Elisha stretched his body upon the little boy. In a little while, the deathly cold flesh of the child began to get warm again. Elisha got up and walked around the house for a while, then went back into the chamber and stretched his body out upon the child again. This time the little boy sneezed several times and opened his eyes.

Elisha called for the woman to come into the room. "Here's your son," he said. "Pick him up!" And she did. (See 2 Kings 4:30–37.)

The devil will always try to take away your blessing and erode your faith. But when you are in the will of God, you can be sure that it shall be well! When God blesses you out of love—because it is His will to bless you—He will keep you . . . and what He has given to you. You can count on it.

Speaking about His followers—His sheep—Jesus said, "And I give unto them eternal life; and they shall never perish, neither shall any man pluck them out of my hand. My Father, which gave them me, is greater than all; and no man is able to pluck them out of my Father's hand" (John 10:28–29).

One of the saddest Scripture passages I know comes toward the end of the Gospels. Jesus is pictured near the end of His earthly ministry, shortly before the events leading up to the Crucifixion. He had come to proclaim a heavenly kingdom to God's chosen people, the Jews, which included the opportunity for a more personal, intimate relationship with God. But the only savior they wanted to receive was a political leader, a military champion who would drive their Roman rulers out of the country and return their lives to the previous status quo. So, except for a relatively small percentage of people who followed Jesus and heard Him teach, most of the people of Israel—and especially the leaders—rejected Him.

So as Jesus was coming into Jerusalem, the nation's capital, for one of the last times He looked out over the city and cried, "O Jerusalem, Jerusalem . . . how often would I have gathered thy children together, even as a hen gathereth her chickens under her wings, and ye would not!" (Matt. 23:37).

Why didn't it happen? Was Jesus able to do it? Oh, yes, He was able. Was He willing? Yes, indeed—willing and eager to have personal fellowship and to provide for them. The problem was with the people. They were "choked with cares and riches and pleasures of this life" (Luke 8:14). Their faith was shortcircuited. It was inoperative. It was going nowhere.

Now, getting back to the leper, I suggest to you that this man did not have faith just because he heard about Jesus. I believe that somewhere in this man's spirit, he always believed he could overcome his circumstances. He just needed to make the connection. This man refused to be imprisoned and enslaved by his mentality. He did not see himself as a leper! He saw himself made whole and set free!

I believe the reason some people are not healed—cannot be healed—is that they simply cannot see themselves whole. Remember the woman with the issue of blood. After twelve years of suffering, of spending all her money on doctors, she still did not see herself as a hopeless case. "If I can just touch the hem of Jesus' garment," she said, "I will be made whole." She saw herself being healed. That's what she was looking for, expecting!

A SLAVE MENTALITY
SHORTCIRCUITS FAITH

THE REASON men and women do not receive what they need from God today has nothing to do with the ability of God to meet their need. *He is able.* And it has nothing to do with His will to meet their need. *He is willing.* The problem is their own mentality that cannot accept what God is so eager to give. They are bound by their own attitudes. They are enslaved by the picture they see of themselves.

It is the will of God that no person have a slave mentality, whether male or female, rich or poor, whether white, black, brown, or yellow. The slave mentality has nothing to do with your gender or your color. It's the way you see yourself.

Daniel and the three Hebrew children—Shadrach, Meshach, and Abednego—were part of the nation of Judah that was defeated in battle and carried away into slavery into Persia. The remarkable thing is that while the vast majority of the Jews developed a slave mentality, doing exactly what their masters ordered them to do, Daniel didn't. He continued to pray to God three times a day with his window opened so he could look toward Jerusalem. And he continued his practice even when he knew the king had signed a decree forbidding prayer. Daniel was a free man inside, not a slave.

Shadrach, Meshach, and Abednego refused to bow down to the king's golden idol, although apparently all the rest of the Jews were violating their conscience and the law of God to do so. The three young men refused to give in, choosing to obey God rather than man, despite the consequences of the fiery furnace. They understood what true liberty was.

During the awful years of World War II, when Hitler, Mussolini, and the Nazis slaughtered some six million Jews in an unspeakable holocaust, a pitiful few of the Jewish people managed to escape the concentration camps and the ovens. Their countries were destroyed, their homes and businesses taken, their reputations despoiled, their bodies abused. They suffered perhaps the worst persecution the world has ever known. Yet they refused to give up. Their will to live did not waver. They experienced an inner liberty their persecutors could never understand.

More than a century ago, great numbers of African people were taken from their homeland and brought to America to become slaves. Although kept in chains, branded like cattle, and treated like animals, many of these people refused to accept their condition. They refused to see themselves as slaves. They might have been at the mercy of the plantation owners and their cruel taskmasters. They might have lived in shacks and shanties and been forced to work long hours in the hot sun, burning up their lives in the fields, but they never forgot where they came from or who they really were. They never forgot what it was like to be free.

Several years ago Alex Haley wrote a book that told the story of slavery in America. This book became a television documentary entitled *Roots*. The main character in the story was a man named Kunta Kinta, who experienced all the hardship and sorrow of the black people in the south. But he never accepted his lot as a slave. And he never developed a slave mentality.

There are too many people today who have

gradually accepted the shackles of bondage and given up their freedom. They have forgotten their rights and privileges as people of liberty and have developed a slave mentality. No, I'm not talking about the slavery that disgraced this country in the 1800s. I'm not talking about political bondage that keeps millions of people enslaved to this day in scores of countries around the world.

There is a slavery worse than these, and more widespread. It is the slavery of Satan, the great deceiver. It is the bondage of the devil that warps people's minds and links them to sin, sorrow, and evil, keeping them from becoming the people God wants and intends them to be.

God doesn't want us to have a slave mentality. When the church was born, it was birthed in power and authority. With the outpouring of the Holy Spirit came freedom and liberty for all, and the anointing to act as ambassadors for Christ.

But the church today has lost its first love. The church is in love with creeds and doctrines, with traditions and rituals, with possessions and property, with prestige and respectability. The church is in love with everything except the Lord Jesus Christ and His will and purpose.

The church no longer asks, "Lord, what is Your will? What would You have us to be? What would You have us to do?" How long has it been, do you suppose, since the people who make up the body of the church have presented their "bodies a living sacrifice, holy, acceptable unto God, which is [their] reasonable service" (Rom. 12:1)?

Turning from God to ourselves, little by little we have taken on the bonds of slavery. Our minds have been taken over by self, by sin, by the flesh, by the world, and by the devil. We no longer see ourselves victorious and free.

But God comes to take the shackles off your mind. He comes to cleanse you from every spot of leprosy that causes you to be an outcast of society. He comes to free your mind, to liberate you, and to set you free. He is saying, "If God be for you, who can be against you?" (See Romans 8:31.)

FAITH BRINGS
DELIVERANCE AND FREEDOM

WE NEED to turn willingly to Jesus today. He is our source of true freedom. The Bible says, "If the Son therefore shall make you free, ye shall be free indeed" (John 8:36). We need to see God . . . and experience the power of God. He alone is able to break the shackles of sin and destroy the bondage of Satan. He alone can lead us out of our slave mentality and cause us to shout, "Free at last! Free at last! Thank God Almighty, I'm free at last!"

God is able. But that's not all.

God is willing.

We know that He is able, that He has all power. But He is also willing. He wants to bless you, meet your needs, and set you free. So let God have your burden. Let Him have your misery. Let God have your oppressive circumstances. He is able to deliver you. And He is willing!

The God of your salvation is willing. Jesus, the Savior of the world, is willing. Jesus, the Head of the church, is willing. Jesus, the Healer who healeth all thy diseases and taketh sickness from the midst of you—He is willing. Jesus, your High Priest, who invites you to cast all your cares on Him, is willing. He is willing "to do exceeding abundantly above all that [you] ask or think" (Eph. 3:20), by the power of God that is in you. He is willing.

The God I serve is a mighty God. He is the eternal God. He is a faithful God. And He is willing!

Now, Lord, here we are in Your presence. Oh, God, we know that when we pray, You will answer. Right now as I speak, I ask You to release Yourself to this friend. I invite You in as the Savior. Save lost women, men, boys, and girls from their sins. Wash away the mark of death and make them over into new creations, fresh, whole, and righteous in Your sight. O God, You are the convicting power of the Holy Ghost. Convict people of sin and convince them of their need for You.

Give us Your salvation, Lord, in the name of Jesus. Oh God, we stand as broken vessels. We need the infilling of the blessed Holy Spirit. We need a new baptism. We need a new anointing. We need You to put Your hand on us, O God. We need You to breathe on us, to quicken us from the dead things of this world. We need You, O God, to overshadow us and take control of our lives. Put Your hand of healing on the sick today. Let them feel the power of God, for You have already borne their sicknesses and their diseases in Your body, on Calvary's tree. By Your stripes, we have already been healed. We invite You in as our Healer today. We say, "Yes, Lord." We cling to You, Jesus. Only You, Lord, do we love. And we shall serve You all the days of our lives. Thank You for hearing me today. Amen.

Chapter Four

Don't Let Satan
Steal Your Faith

THE ENEMY of your soul is also the archenemy of God Himself. We have an alliance with God that came by repenting of our sins, denouncing the flesh, the world, and the devil, and by receiving Jesus as Lord. As a result of that alliance, God's friends are our friends, and His enemies are our enemies. So because of our love for God and our alliance with Him, Satan is out to destroy us.

The Bible says, "Your adversary the devil, as a roaring lion, walketh about, seeking whom he may devour" (1 Pet. 5:8). The apostle Paul wrote, "For we are not ignorant of his devices" (2 Cor. 2:11), for he is able to masquerade himself as "an angel of light" (2 Cor. 11:14). But Satan is the enemy of our souls.

If you are going to live this life, you must know your enemy and be prepared for spiritual warfare. And you must be aware that this is not just a weekend war. The battle is not fought just on Sunday, but every day of your life.

Paul says in 2 Corinthians 10:3–4, "For though we [the church] walk in the flesh, we do not war after the flesh: For the weapons of our warfare are not carnal, but mighty through God to the pulling down of strongholds." God has given us weapons so we can be victorious. One of the main weapons in our arsenal that must be used consistently is faith. To my mind, it is perhaps the most important weapon of all.

I realize that some may not agree. Many would probably say love is the essential mark of the believer, and his chief weapon. The Bible certainly emphasizes the importance of love, declaring that "God is love" (1 John 4:8). And Paul even writes about "faith which worketh by love" (Gal. 5:6). I recognize that truth. But it is still faith that is doing the work.

The Bible says, "But the fruit of the Spirit is love, joy, peace, longsuffering, gentleness, goodness, faith, meekness, temperance" (Gal. 5:22–23). Love and faith are included in this list of truly excellent qualities that help make up and express the Spirit-filled life. And God wants us to exhibit all the fruit of the Spirit.

"But without faith it is impossible to please [God]: for he that cometh to God must believe that he is, and that he is a rewarder of them that diligently seek him" (Heb. 11:6). Faith is what pleases God. And Satan is trying to steal your faith. If he can steal your faith, he can destroy you.

The devil is a destroyer. The strategy of hell is to take away your joy, to rob you of peace, to render you ineffective in the Kingdom of God. The devil wants to steal your faith. He is after your husband. He is after your wife. He is after your children. He's after your job, your business. He's after your financial security. He's after your happiness.

Jesus said, "The thief cometh not, but for to steal, and to kill, and to destroy. . . ." Thank God, He didn't stop there. The last part of that verse provides us protection against the devil's evil intentions and destructive attacks. Jesus went on to say, "I am come that they might have life, and that they might have it more abundantly" (John 10:10).

The first man, Adam, was created by the hand of God and made perfect and whole. He had the life of God within him, and was clothed in the righteousness of God. He had dominion and control of all God's creation. Then came temptation, and Adam sinned. When he violated God's will, the righteousness of God could not dwell in him, and the life of God departed. Sin stripped him naked and rendered him ineffective. And the man who once had been given divine dominion became the dominated. Man became a tool in the hands of the serpent.

But before sin could even raise its ugly head in triumph, God introduced His remedy for sin. He prophetically declared that the seed of the woman would bruise the head of the serpent. (See Genesis 3:15.) He promised that mankind would be redeemed.

Adam waited for that promise, and so did his son Abel. Abraham looked for the fulfillment of that prophetic word of God, as did Isaac, Jacob, and Joseph. *The generations rolled by.* Moses fought great battles against the forces of evil as the spiritual warfare continued. *And time went by.* Throughout the Old Testament, we read of great heroes like Gideon, Samson, David, Samuel, and the prophets, all still waiting for God's remedy for sin and the redemption of mankind from the fall.

GOD SENT HIS SON TO DESTROY THE WORKS OF THE DEVIL

THE BIBLE SAYS, "When the fulness of the time was come . . . ." Oh, yes, centuries had gone by, but God had not forgotten. He waited until the time was right . . . until His time had come.

Then, "God sent forth his Son, made of a woman, made under the law, to redeem them that were under the law" (Gal. 4:4–5). Jesus came to earth—born of a woman, made under the law. He looked like a man. He walked like a man. He talked like a man. He *was* a man—but a very special man, the Son of God! Incorporated within Him was God Himself. "In the beginning was the Word, and the Word was with God, and the Word was God" (John 1:1). Jesus was *very* man and *very* God!

Jesus came to do warfare with Satan. John testified, "For this purpose the Son of God was manifested, that he might destroy the works of the devil" (1 John 3:8).

As the Lord prepared to carry out His earthly mission, He went to be baptized by John. And Luke's Gospel tells us that as He stood praying in the Jordan River, the heavens opened up. If you're going to go out and do spiritual warfare, you'd better learn to pray. If you need a touch from God, you need to pray. When you pray, God will visit you. He will reveal Himself to you. He will surround you with His presence. He will touch you, bless you, empower you. And whatever you need, God will grant it to you.

When Jesus prayed, heaven was opened, "And the Holy Ghost descended in a bodily shape like a dove upon him, and a voice came from heaven, which said, Thou art my beloved Son; in thee I am well pleased" (Luke 3:22). Have you prayed until heaven's doors opened up to you? Have you prayed until the Holy Ghost came down and filled you with power and joy?

Have you prayed until you heard from God and knew you were in His will?

After His baptism, the Bible says the Spirit of God drove Jesus into the wilderness to be tempted by Satan. He started out by fasting for forty days and nights. The Bible says that afterward He was hungry. That's when the devil's temptations started. Satan loves to use our appetites and desires to get us into trouble.

The devil said to Jesus, "I know You must be hungry. So, if You're the Son of God, turn these stones into bread."

Jesus could have done that. All power in heaven and earth was given to Him. It would have been an easy thing to do. But He replied to Satan, "It is written, Man shall not live by bread alone, but by every word that proceedeth out of the mouth of God" (Matt. 4:4).

Do you want to be victorious over the devil? Then make up your mind that you're going to live by every word of God. Not some of the Word. Not part of the Word. Not just the Word that sounds good to you. Not just the Word that's not too strict or not too demanding. You have to decide to live by the Word—every word that comes out of the mouth of God Almighty.

Then the devil took Jesus up on the roof of the temple and said, "If You're the Son of God, jump off this pinnacle and see what happens. There are

supposed to be angels protecting You from even stub-
bing your toe on a rock."

And Jesus replied, "It is written again, Thou shalt
not tempt the Lord thy God" (Matt. 4:7).

Satan tried again. He took Jesus to a lookout point
up on a very high mountain and showed him the glory
and beauty of all the kingdoms of the world. "Let's
make a deal, Jesus. I'll give all these things to You if You
will fall down and worship me."

"Then saith Jesus unto him, Get thee hence, Satan:
for it is written, Thou shalt worship the Lord thy
God, and him only shalt thou serve. Then the devil
leaveth him, and, behold, angels came and ministered
unto him" (Matt. 4:10–11).

The church's sin today is trying to worship God
without serving Him! And it won't work. I'm telling
you, you can *shachah,* you can *barak,* you can *hallel;*
you can perform all of the Hebrew expressions of
worship, but if your heart is not right with God,
your worship is in vain. For your worship to be acceptable, you must also serve God. You must love Him
with all of your heart, all of your soul, all of your mind,
and all of your strength.

Jesus rebuked the hypocritical religious leaders of
His day by saying, "This people draweth nigh unto me
with their mouth, and honoreth me with their lips; but
their heart is far from me" (Matt. 15:8).

The Lord wants our hearts to be connected to His

heart—to be intertwined, intermingled, locked up, tied up, and tangled up with His heart. When your heart is right, you are willing—eager—to serve God, to do His will, to put Him first in your life.

JESUS IS OUR EXAMPLE

JESUS WAS the pattern Son—the great example we can follow. Peter said that Jesus "also suffered for us, leaving us an example, that [we] should follow his steps" (1 Pet. 2:21). And Jesus Himself said, "For I have given you an example, that ye should do as I have done to you" (John 13:15). The Lord showed us that faith is the key to being a productive servant of God.

Paul wrote, "So then faith cometh by hearing, and hearing by the word of God" (Rom. 10:17). Faith is contained in the voice of God Almighty. The written Word, our Holy Bible, was spoken by the Spirit of God to great men of old who wrote it all down. What was created through these writers was more than just a book—it is a powerful expression of God Himself. And every page of this written Word is impregnated and saturated with the faith of God.

When we read the Bible, we read about God. We gain knowledge and information about God—who He is, His history and future, His will and purpose, His love and power. But the written Word is not intended to be our only contact with God. Reading the

Bible imparts information, but not necessarily an experience with God.

The Spirit of God must come to us and move in us to make the written Word come alive. For not only is God the written Word, He is the eternal Word . . . the creative Word . . . the incarnate Word—the Living Word! And when that Word *lives* within us, we hear His Word in our souls and in our hearts. We sense His presence with us, and are aware of His faith empowering us to live our lives for Him. We discover, as Paul expressed it, that "in him we live, and move, and have our being" (Acts 17:28).

The Word is the source and the foundation of faith. And faith is the essential structure of our very lives. Both the Old and New Testaments declare that "the just shall live by faith." (See Habbakuk 2:4; Romans 1:17.)

Faith gets us up in the morning and sustains us throughout the day. Faith gives us courage to walk through the darkest night, and keeps us smiling through weariness and difficulty. Faith rejoices in times of blessing, and is also joyful *in spite of* negative circumstances. Faith is what moves mountains, obtains the unobtainable, and does the impossible.

No wonder the devil is after your faith! If he can't seize it and tear it from your grasp—and he can't— then he'll try to convince you that everything's fine and you can coast. "Just lay your faith down and enjoy life.

You can still make it with God!" Don't be deceived by that lying devil! Hold on to your faith.

Satan never quits trying to steal your faith. If he fails to tear it away from you, and fails to persuade you to lay faith aside voluntarily, he'll try to discourage you. If he can get you overloaded and busy, running here and there, trying to do too much, wearing you down, the pressure starts building up. Getting involved in too many activities and endeavors—even good things—can have a bad effect. When you're worn out and frustrated, you are more vulnerable to feeling dismayed and disheartened by the complications of life. Be careful! Don't let your weakened state make you the prey of Satan.

God wants you to be an overcomer, not a victim. One day when I was feeling weary and discouraged, I turned in my Bible and read something that jumped off the page at me and gave me a surge of excitement and energy. Here it is: "For whatsoever is born of God overcometh the world: and this is the victory that overcometh the world, *even our faith*" (1 John 5:4, emphasis mine).

FAITH IS THE VICTORY

WHAT IS the believer's weapon for victory? Is it love? Is it patience? Is it mercy? No, it's not even grace. *Faith is the victory!* Faith overcomes the world. The

Bible says, "Be strong in the Lord, and in the power of his might. Put on the whole armor of God, that ye may be able to stand against the wiles of the devil. For we wrestle not against flesh and blood, but against principalities, against powers, against the rulers of the darkness of this world, against spiritual wickedness in high places. Wherefore take unto you the whole armor of God, that ye may be able to withstand in the evil day, and having done all, to stand" (Eph. 6:10–13).

The word *stand* in this context does not mean to get up on your feet. It does not mean to be idle, as in to "stand around." It really has the connotation of, after making all possible preparations, "taking a stand." In the military sense, to "stand" means to draw a line in the sand and say to the enemy, "You shall not pass. This is as far as you go!"

The devil has no intention of leaving you alone. He will not allow you to walk through this world without opposition or trouble. Remember, Jesus said, "The thief [the devil] cometh not, but for to steal, and to kill, and to destroy" (John 10:10). That means he is definitely out to get you. Don't make the mistake of ignoring him and hoping he'll go away. You must oppose Satan. You are an active soldier in the army of the Lord. "Be strong in the Lord, and in the power of his might" (Eph. 6:10).

When the devil comes to try and take your wife, take a stand! When he comes to take your husband, draw a line! When he comes to take your children, put him on notice that you're ready to fight. When Satan tries to steal your house, your car, your prosperity, your health, your peace—don't give up anything!

David's "Giant Faith"

THE BOOK of 1 Samuel tells the familiar story of the shepherd boy David and his battle with the giant warrior Goliath. David came out to the battlefield to visit his three brothers who were soldiers in the army of Israel. He was expecting to see a battle raging. But there was no fighting going on at all.

The Philistine champion, Goliath, came out periodically to challenge the army of Israel to send out a fighting man to do battle with him. This giant, perhaps nine to ten feet tall, was covered from head to toe with heavy armor that protected him from arrows, spears, and the blows of any challenger. He cursed and jeered the army of Israel, and intimidated them with his threats.

David was amazed to see Israel's entire army cowering in fear, including Saul, the king, who stood head and shoulders above all his troops. "Why is nobody responding to this big bully?" David wanted to know.

His brothers were angry with him. "You don't know what you're talking about. Why don't you go back to the sheep? You're just a kid who came out to see a fight."

"Well, I don't see any fight going on," said David. "And I'm not afraid to fight. When a lion came against my sheep, I fought and killed the beast. And the same with a bear who tried to steal a lamb. I killed the bear also. And I'm not afraid of this arrogant Philistine who has defied the army of the living God."

Then someone told David that the king had offered a reward to any man who would respond to Goliath's challenge. If the man was successful in destroying the giant, he would be given the king's daughter in marriage, be awarded great riches, and his father's household would be freed from taxes. David said, "That sounds good to me! Where do I sign up?"

Someone ran to tell Saul that there was a volunteer ready to go fight Goliath. Soon David was telling his story to the king about killing the lion and the bear, and sharing with Saul that he was confident the Lord would deliver the enemy's giant into his hand. After worrying about David's youth and inexperience, Saul finally agreed to let the young man be the representative for Israel against Goliath. After all, no one else would do it. "You can fight the battle," said Saul, "but you have to wear my armor."

"What for?" was David's reply. "It doesn't seem to have been doing you any good! No, I'll go fight the battle in my own way, with my own weapons. I didn't use armor and a shield to kill the lion and the bear. And I can't go out against Goliath with your weapons.

I can't trust in your testimony. I'll go out in the strength and power of my own faith. And I'll just take along this handful of rocks and my slingshot!"

Can't you imagine what the soldiers of Israel must have been saying as David got ready to fight. "Who does he think he is, anyhow? He's too ignorant to even know what's going to happen when Goliath gets his hands on him. David hasn't got a chance. He's going to get killed, sure as the world."

But David paid them no mind. He took his shepherd's staff and his sling and jogged out onto the battlefield to face the giant who had just come out to taunt Israel again. When Goliath saw this unarmed seventeen-year-old shepherd boy coming out to face him, he was enraged. "What am I, a dog, that you come out against me with a stick? I curse you by the gods of the Philistines, and if you come any closer, I will feed you to the birds." (See 1 Samuel 17:43–44.)

When he heard that, David started running straight toward the giant. "You come against me with a sword and a spear, but I come to you in the name of the Lord, the God of Israel, whom you have defied. The Lord will give you into my hand, and I will take your head off and feed the carcasses of your soldier buddies to the beasts. For the battle is the Lord's!"

When Goliath charged, David took a single stone and put it into his slingshot. He whirled the sling around his head and threw the rock with all his might.

The stone made a perfect arc and struck Goliath in the one small spot that was unprotected by armor—where the visor was raised so he could see. The stone smashed into his forehead and killed him instantly. By the time Goliath's huge body had crumpled onto the ground, David had run to his side and drawn the giant's huge sword. With one mighty blow he decapitated him.

Seeing their champion fall, the Philistines reacted in terror and turned to flee. But they were unprepared and disorganized, and soon the soldiers of Israel came rushing into the camp, weapons at the ready. A great slaughter began and continued until the entire Philistine army was destroyed. Through David's faith in God, Israel won a great battle that day.

USE YOUR FAITH TO DEFEAT THE DEVIL

YOU HAVE authority in the Word of God. As a child of God, you have power in the blood of Christ and life in the Spirit of God. You have a weapon that causes the devil to back up every time! When you wield the sword of the Spirit, Satan must retreat. You can oppose him in Jesus' name and remind him that the battle is the Lord's! He can't win. The victory is already won. Your faith will protect you and enable you to overcome every fiery dart of the enemy.

But you must be bold and strong. You have to become violent! The Bible says, "The kingdom of heaven suffereth violence, and the violent take it by force" (Matt. 11:12). None of this weak mumbling and bumbling about. Open your mouth and declare what you want—in faith believing. God has given you power through His Spirit, through the Holy Ghost, through the power of His blood. You will not fail. You cannot be defeated. There is no failure or defeat in God.

Victory does not depend on your size or strength, or your skill as a fighter. This is a spiritual battle—a continuation of the age-old struggle between God and the devil. And God is on your side. So you don't have to run, or cry, or tremble in fear. You don't have to worry about the outcome. Just stand still and see the salvation of your God. He will fight for you, and He will win the battle.

Don't let the devil steal your faith. You can be an overcomer. You can resist the enemy's attacks with tenacity and determination. You can defeat him and make him flee. Pick up your faith. Use your faith. Be ready to do spiritual warfare with Satan. You can march forward with confidence, knowing that you have a secret weapon that guarantees you the victory. What is it?

The beloved apostle John said, "Ye are of God, little children, and have overcome [Satan]: because greater is he that is in you, than he that is in the world" (1 John 4:4).

CHAPTER FIVE

NO WEAPON FORMED
AGAINST YOU SHALL PROSPER

HERE'S A PROMISE from the Word of God that you can hold on to. Here's a truth that will take you through the tough times when you feel like there's a target painted on your back and all your enemies are shooting at you—that Satan and all his demons are on your trail! The Bible says, "No weapon that is formed against thee shall prosper . . . This is the heritage of the servants of the Lord" (Isa. 54:17).

Here are several things about this promise that you need to give special consideration. *First,* the prophet said this promise is the heritage of the *servants* of the Lord. What does this mean? Simply this—if you're not a servant of the Lord, disregard this promise! If you're not serving God, you don't qualify for this benefit.

What does it mean to serve God? It means to *listen* to the voice of God, pay attention to what He says, and then to do whatever He tells you to do.

Now, if you're not serving God and you get in trouble, don't come around asking God why things went wrong. Go talk to your daddy, the devil! If you're serving Satan, try complaining to him about your worries and hurts and problems.

Second, if you are serving God, be sure you understand what the promise is. The Bible doesn't say no weapon will be formed against you. That's not what it says at all! Believe me, when you come to Jesus and begin to follow Him, the weapons *are* formed against you. The devil puts you on his hit list! You are targeted. Don't you ever think that because you're born again and living for Christ you are immune and shielded from all opposition.

If you're God's servant, weapons have been formed against you. The fiery darts of the wicked are already being aimed your way!

Peter said, "Beloved, think it not strange concerning the fiery trial which is to try you, as though some strange thing happened unto you: but rejoice, inasmuch as ye are partakers of Christ's sufferings; that, when his glory shall be revealed, ye may be glad also with exceeding joy" (1 Pet. 4:12–13).

What does the promise in Isaiah say? It says, "No weapon that is formed against thee *shall prosper!*" The weapon will be formed, but it won't thrive, or bloom, or flourish. No weapon formed against you *will succeed!*

Oh, yes, the devil will form a weapon of financial pressure against you, but because you are serving God, He will supply your need. The devil will launch the weapon of strife and unrest against your household, but God will honor your faithful service and speak peace upon your family. The devil will bring sickness and disease, fear and calamities to your house, but no weapon formed against you will prosper and succeed! No matter what men may try to do against you, God will help you withstand every attack, win every battle, come through every trial, overcome every difficulty and discouragement.

I know, when things start going wrong, you have some friends who'll gather around and say, "My, my, you must be out of the will of God. Looks like you're being punished for your sins and shortcomings. If you were right with God, surely you wouldn't be having so much trouble!" Don't you believe it! That's a lie of the devil. Do you remember the accusations of Job's "comforters?" Even his wife turned on him and said, "Why don't you just curse God and die!"

Too many church members today don't understand that faith is *not* a vaccination that will keep them from catching trouble ever again. They want to get saved, go to church for a one-hour, "feel good" service on Sunday morning, and live happily ever after until it's time to go to heaven!

So when the devil forms a weapon against them, they panic. When trouble comes their way, they're not ready for it.

The devil, as a roaring lion, comes into their back yard, seeking to devour them, and they have a heart attack right there! They throw up their hands and cry, "Oh, poor me. My God, what am I going to do? I'm so alone! Why did God abandon me?"

The first hardship that comes their way overwhelms them. They fall down and start having a pity party all by themselves. The next thing you know they've quit coming to church. They quit associating with people who know God, who fast and pray and study the Word, who testify about what God can do, and can encourage them in the Lord.

Instead of throwing up their hands at the first sign of opposition, they start associating with the people in the church who are lukewarm and indifferent. They hang around with that bunch that doesn't worship, doesn't give, doesn't have anything, and doesn't do anything. And before long, they drop out altogether.

WHOSE SERVANT ARE YOU?

THE BIBLE says the heritage of God's servants is that no

weapon formed against them shall prosper. So if the weapons are prospering—if the weapons are succeeding—what does that say? We have to take a look at whose servants they really are, don't we? It really does not matter what an individual claims to be if they're not *living* it. The apostle James said, "Faith without works is dead" (2:20).

The Book of Acts tells about the seven sons of Sceva, who were called "vagabond Jews." They tried to cast the evil spirits out of a man, not through their own experience with God, but "by Jesus whom Paul preacheth" (19:13). The evil spirit responded, "Jesus I know, and Paul I know; but who are ye?" (v. 15). Now look what happened next—"And the man in whom the evil spirit was leaped on them [all seven of them], and overcame them, and prevailed against them, so that they fled out of that house naked and wounded" (Acts 19:16).

God's promise is for His people—His servants. And it says that no weapon, no missile, no Sherman tank, no AK47, no .38, no .22, no ballistic missile, no bazooka, no hand grenade—"No weapon that is formed against thee shall prosper . . . This is the heritage of the servants of the Lord" (Isa. 54:17).

The key focus in this text is not upon the fact that no weapon formed against you will prosper! That's what folks shout about, but that's not the key. There is a *condition* to be met before that clause is in effect. The condition is: *You must be a servant of the Lord.* The key to having no weapon *succeed* against you is *to serve the Lord.*

The psalmist David said, "I am a servant of the Lord, and what's more, I 'serve the Lord with gladness' (Ps. 100:2)." David woke up every morning with a desire burning deep within his breast to enter into the presence of God. He said, "I was glad when they said unto me, Let us go into the house of the Lord" (Ps. 122:1).

There's something about God's house that is different from any other house. That difference isn't the style of architecture—a high roofline, a steeple, or stained-glass windows. The difference isn't the shape or placement of the podium at which a minister stands to speak. The thing that makes a building God's house is the presence of the Lord is there!

There are buildings that have all the outward appearances of a church, and inside various religious functions and church activities appear to be going on. Men with theological and divinity degrees speak from much study and learning, but there is something absent from their message. They provide information, but there's no life to their messages. They have the letter of the Word, but the Bible says "the letter killeth, but the spirit giveth life" (2 Cor. 3:6).

When you visit this kind of church, you sense an emptiness in the facility they occupy. Everything is there . . . except the presence of God. And that's the important thing.

God is not attracted to facilities or pleasing architecture. He is attracted to hearts that are open to Him and people who worship Him in Spirit and in truth. When we open our hearts to God and pour out our very being on the altar of sacrifice before Him, that attracts God. That will get His attention. Then He will come and get involved in our worship, and we will have an encounter with Him.

An Encounter With God

Have you ever had an encounter with God? When God called me to preach, I was at home, praying and seeking the Lord. Suddenly the Spirit of God dramatically swept over me, and I fell to the floor. Although I'd never been to a church where people were "slain in the Spirit," it happened to me while I was all by myself. I knew it was God. I was laying there, and when I tried to get up, I couldn't move. Here was God Almighty, the Creator of heaven and earth, my Lord, my Redeemer— literally sitting on me. And I could not get up.

If you want to be a servant of the Lord, you have to let God sit on you. You want Him to sit there until He gets through doing all that He wants to do in your life. Whatever He's begun in you, let Him complete it. Let Him remove anything in your life that's unholy, unclean, impure, and not Christ-like. Learn to cry out and say, "Oh God, do something in my life. Change the things that are making my heart harden toward You." When God sits on you, stay there and let Him work. Don't get in a hurry to get up. Stay in His presence until God gets done with what He wants to do in your life.

I'm of the opinion that you can't have church in forty-five minutes. By then you're just getting warmed up. Some of us are so cold it takes that long just to get ready to worship. The devil has been trying us all week long, and it takes forty-five minutes just to get our minds off our problems, off ourselves, and onto God. Only then can we expect heaven to open and the Spirit of God to come and do His work.

You get heaven open by walking in righteousness. Then you allow the Spirit of God to come in the form of a dove and to abide in your life. See, the Holy Ghost doesn't come to drive you; He comes to lead you. When the Holy Ghost is come, God will testify to you that "this is my beloved Son, in whom I am well pleased" (Matt. 3:17). There were hundreds of people at John's baptism, but heaven was opened to one man only. Only one man received the empowerment, the endowment, the baptism, the cover, the energizing of the Holy Ghost, the enablement of God.

Countless weapons have been formed against me—but none of them have stuck to me. People have called me everything but a child of God. People inside and outside of the church have plotted to destroy me, but

I'm still here. Why? Because I want to do God's will. I want to be His servant. I give my life for His purpose and His use. So no weapon formed against me can prosper and succeed.

FAITH FULFILLS THE WILL OF GOD IN PORT CHESTER, NEW YORK

THE LORD led me to pastor my first church in Port Chester, New York, a small transient community. I rented some space in a little storefront building from a Jewish fellow who had an ongoing legal battle against the village of Port Chester. He also ran a small village newspaper, which most of the time concentrated on reporting the real dirty stuff that went on in the village.

I wasn't interested in any of that. All I wanted was to start a church. When I inquired about putting up a sign, someone told me I needed a permit from the village. When I went to get the permit at the village office, the supervisor who was working there asked me, "Where do you want to hang the sign—what is the address?"

When I told him, he said, "Oh, you can't do that. We have a law on the books that prohibits any church being open in the village of Port Chester unless it owns an acre of land and has plenty of on-site parking." Now, in New York that much property would cost more than a million dollars.

I said, "You can't enforce that law. That's unconstitutional."

And the guy said, "Well, you'd have to prove that . . . and nobody has. And we're not going to give you a permit."

"That's discrimination," I said, and I signed up to be on the agenda for the village council meeting that night.

I arrived and waited through the council's usual routine business, waiting for my turn to speak. But they never called me. When I saw that the mayor was about to dismiss the meeting, I stood up and interrupted him. I said, "I had a request before the village, and I'm sure you have it on your agenda. I'm asking for a variance to open a church here."

He said, "Well, it's here, but we've already made a decision that we're not going to grant your request."

I said, "So you're not going to even give me a hearing?"

He said, "No."

So very calmly I said to him, "Have you ever read in the Bible about the people who withstood Moses—that there was death in every house?"

All of a sudden war broke out. You could see the anger in every one of these guys. They were up front, and I was in the back, and all of us were speaking very loudly. Reporters from the newspapers were there, paying close attention to what was going on.

I said, "Well, the Lord sent me here to open a church, and I'm going to do it, permit or no permit."

The next day the newspaper reported on the fireworks at the council meeting. The main headline was "David Takes On Goliath!" There was a real controversy, with continuing newspaper articles. The guy I rented the building from began to promote me heavily in his paper. We were at odds with the entire village. The controversy got so ugly that the city manager declared that if anybody went into our church, the village would put them in jail. But I kept opening the church, and people came. The threats encouraged rather than stopped the people from coming.

Sadly, I couldn't get one pastor in that community to help me—not one—although the controversy went on for about six months. But the Lord helped me.

About the seventh month, the newspaper did another story on me. The reporter who interviewed me asked, "Are you aware that the city manager said if you were not out of here soon, he was going to put you in jail?"

"I don't believe I'm going to jail," I replied.

The reporter went directly to the city manager to get his response to my words. "Well, I guess it's time for us to put out a warrant for his arrest," the city manager stated.

The next Sunday, Jeremiah Goodman, a Jewish man who worked for the ACLU, appeared in my church. He said, "We're here to help you. The next time the village threatens you, we're going to take them to court."

Sure enough, a week later the village threatened to close the church and to put me in jail. That evening Jeremiah Goodman called me and said, "Be at the village office in the morning at eight o'clock."

I was there. Goodman had gotten a restraining order citing the New York state constitution. He also filed a lawsuit for $125,000. It was amazing how quickly the village backed down. They immediately made the concession and gave me a variance. The next day the newspapers reported, "Goliath Is Defeated . . . and Rev. Andrew Merritt Wins!" Nobody had ever taken on this village before, but God directed me to put up a fight.

After that I was accepted. The village leaders invited me to be on every committee they could find to put me on. I was included in lots of village functions and activities. And our church was established and began to grow.

Don't misunderstand. The victory was not because of me. The power did not come from me! I succeeded through the power of faith in God. The reason I am who I am today is because of God. I was created in God before the foundation of the world. And I have come to the kingdom of God for such a time as this. I'm on schedule. I didn't come before my time. I'm here in season. And because of that, no weapon formed against me will succeed. If someone hired a hit man to take me out, he'd wind up shooting himself! There's no other preacher in this city, in this state, in this nation, in this world, who can do what I'm supposed to do. God called me to be His servant at Straight Gate Church, and nobody else can or will do what God created me to accomplish.

You see, God chose me—I didn't choose Him. It is He who has made us, and not we ourselves! God chose you—you didn't choose Him. Though you were dead in trespasses and sin, He *quickened* you—He made you alive! (See Ephesians 2:1.)

God is doing something in your life that is far greater than you can imagine. He is not just delivering you from firearms and drugs, from crack cocaine, and from murder. Every day we read of people who die just walking through our cities. Yet you walk those mean streets, and you're still here by the mercy of God. Why?

You have a work to perform. You have a will to conform to. God wants to use you. God wants to work mightily in you. "For it is God which worketh in you both to will and to do of his good pleasure" (Phil. 2:13). God wants to overshadow you. He wants to breathe on you. He wants to anoint you. He wants you to preach. He wants you to teach. He wants you to witness.

God didn't save you to come to church and sit up front and say "Amen." He didn't save you for Sunday morning services. He saved you to be His servant—to know His will and to declare His counsel.

Thank God that "I know whom I have believed"

103

(2 Tim. 1:12), and I know who I serve. "But thou, O Lord, art a shield for me; my glory, and the lifter up of mine head" (Ps. 3:3). He sent angels to be around me. "The Lord is my light and my salvation; whom shall I fear? The Lord is the strength of my life; of whom shall I be afraid?" (Ps. 27:1).

Victory in a Fiery Trial

When I was starting out in the ministry years ago, I was a youth pastor in Detroit, Michigan. Not only did I have responsibilities with the young people, I helped conduct the main worship services and handled all the preliminaries. One Saturday night I woke up at 3:00 in the morning and felt thirsty. I got up and went downstairs to get a glass of water. That had never happened to me before, but I got myself a drink and started back up to my bed. Suddenly I smelled smoke! When I got back to the upstairs hall, there were billows of smoke rolling down. The house was on fire!

We called in the alarm, and the firefighters came. Everyone in the house got out safely, and we were standing around in pajamas and bathrobes, wondering how much damage was being done. After a couple hours, the firemen said the problem was caused by faulty electrical wiring. We would not be able to stay there. They would allow us to get some clothes and a few possessions from the house, but then we had to leave.

When I went up to my room, everything was soaked. The firemen had cut a hole in the ceiling of my room because the fire was in the attic directly over my head. They'd poured the water up there, and it had soaked back down into my closet. All my clothes were wet, soggy, and soppy—everything. I knew I had to go to church in a little while to stand in front of the congregation and lead the service. I started praising God and saying, "Thank You, Jesus! Glory to God! Thank You for waking me up and getting me out of this burning house safely. Hallelujah!"

My suits, shirts, and ties were wet, and my shoes were full of water. All the clothes I owned were in that closet, drowned from the fire hoses.

The devil said to me, "There's just no way you can make it to church today. All your clothes are spoiled, and besides, you've had a traumatic experience. No one would expect you to show up after what you've been through."

As I looked around the room, I saw the work clothes that I hadn't put away in the closet—a pair of khaki pants, a blue work shirt, and some big combat boots. I scrounged around for a tie that wasn't too wet, and located a jacket I could pull over the rough work shirt. I said, "Praise God, I'm going to church. I'll wear what I have and give the Lord the praise. Hallelujah!"

"Surely you're not thinking of going into the pulpit wearing khaki pants and combat boots," the devil said, trying to intimidate me. "You can't get up in front of the people with a dirty shirt, a wrinkled tie, and that old, tattered jacket!"

"You just watch me, Devil!" I said.

In the service that morning we sang the words, "We gather together to ask the Lord's blessings . . . " While the congregation was singing this traditional Thanksgiving hymn, I was crying. I couldn't stop crying. People looked at me, probably thinking I was a little strange. They didn't know what God had just done for me. They didn't understand that the Lord had already blessed me in an overwhelming way.

In the regular order of service, following the last song, the leader of the service was supposed to share a short meditation right before the pastor came to preach. But that morning I wasn't going to talk just about the meaning of a song—I had to praise God for what He had done in my life the night before. So I testified about how the devil had formed a weapon against me in the form of an electrical fire to burn the house down. But because I was a servant of God—doing what He told me to do—that weapon didn't prosper. It didn't flourish. It didn't succeed!

That Saturday night I had prayed and laid down to sleep in Jesus' name. In the middle of the night when the devil's fiery weapon was directed against me, God woke me up. The Lord got me up in Jesus' name.

He preserved me in His name.

He delivered me in His name!

And I stood up in that church the next morning, wearing old work clothes, a ragged jacked, a wrinkled tie, with old, rough combat boots on my feet before all the people who were dressed in their Sunday morning best. But my heart was full of praise and thanksgiving. I proclaimed to the people that God is a good God. I told them that I knew for a fact that no weapon formed against us would prosper if we were serving God! I said, "He will take care of us. He will bless us coming in and bless us going out. He'll bless us laying down, and He'll bless us rising up! Blessed be the name of the Lord."

THE FAITHFUL PRAYERS OF DANIEL

THE CONCEPT of God's blessing upon His faithful, praying followers is hard for some people to comprehend. The carnal mind just doesn't understand it. But it works. The Old Testament tells the story of a Jew named Daniel who was a captive in Persia. Even there he was faithful to pray to the Lord three times a day. Daniel's enemies went to Darius, the king of Persia, and convinced him to issue a decree stating that no one was to pray to anyone but the king for thirty days. Anyone who violated this law would be thrown into a den of vicious, hungry lions.

The Persian newspapers ran headline stories about the king's new law. The news spread throughout the kingdom. Everybody was talking about it on the street. Daniel soon heard the report that no one could pray except to the king—upon penalty of death. What did he do?

The Bible says, "Now when Daniel knew that the writing was signed, he went into his house; and his windows being open in his chamber toward Jerusalem, he kneeled upon his knees three times a day, and prayed, and gave thanks before his God, as he did aforetime" (Dan. 6:10). Nothing changed for Daniel. He kept on serving God, obeying God, praying to God.

Daniel's enemies were waiting outside his house to see if he would obey the king's law, or if he would keep praying to his God. As soon as they heard him crying out to the Lord, they ran off to the king's house. "You signed a decree, Mr. King, that no one could pray to anyone but yourself. Well, guess what? Daniel is over there praying to his God! Your decree says the punishment for not obeying is that the offender will be thrown into the lion's den. So Daniel has to die!"

The king was sick at heart about this because he liked and respected Daniel. He knew he could trust Daniel's honesty and wisdom, and had put him in a place of great authority. But now Daniel's enemies had set a trap for both of them. And there was nothing the king could do to save Daniel from the lions.

So they dragged Daniel to the pit, mocking and jeering him. But just before they pushed him over the edge, the king said, "Thy God whom thou servest continually, he will deliver thee" (v. 16).

Did you get it? Do you see it? Daniel was a servant of God! He served God continually! And remember—the promise that "no weapon formed against you shall prosper" is the heritage of the servants of the Lord. Do you believe the promise? Can you stake your life on the faithfulness of God and the truth of His Word? It's hard to do when you're standing at the mouth of a den of hungry lions, and your enemies are ready to shove you in!

That's what they did to Daniel. They threw him into the pit and put a stone across the top with the king's seal on it. Then they walked off with a smirk on their faces, saying, "That's the end of Daniel!"

The king went back to the palace, but he was so upset he couldn't eat or sleep. He was upset that he had allowed Daniel's enemies to trick him. He wanted to believe that Daniel's God could deliver him from being torn apart and eaten by the savage beasts. But he'd heard the growls and snarls of those animals! He'd looked down into that pit and seen their angry, menacing, hungry glares. And he'd never heard of anyone going into the lions' den and coming out alive!

Early the next morning, just as the sun came up, the king hurried back to the lion's den. He walked up to its edge and tried to look in, but he couldn't see anything because of the stone over the opening, with his seal on it, still unbroken.

So the king cried out, "Oh, Daniel, *servant of the living God,* are you down there? Did your God save you from the lions?"

The people standing around snickered under their breath. "Sure, Mr. King. Old Daniel's doing fine. He's still down there . . . inside the bellies of those lions. What did you think would happen?"

The king dropped his head and turned sadly to leave. But wait! What's that sound? "O king, live for ever" (v. 21).

That's Daniel's voice! The king recognized it immediately. Everybody standing around was stunned and astonished. Daniel is alive! He wasn't killed by the lions. How could this be? What's going on here?

"My God hath sent his angel," said Daniel, "and hath shut the lions' mouths, that they have not hurt me" (v. 22).

The king ordered the seal to be broken and the stone taken away from the opening. Then they pulled Daniel out of the lions' den.

Look at what the Bible says—"and no manner of hurt was found upon him, because he believed in his God" (v. 23).

Explain that according to human logic. The hungry lions—the weapon—were there. Daniel—the intended victim—was there, unarmed and helpless. The weapon didn't prosper because Daniel was a servant of the living God! The lions didn't eat that night. The angel of the Lord gave them lockjaw. Daniel didn't have a mark on him. He served God. He believed God. And I wouldn't be surprised to find out that Daniel laid down and slept in peace all night, using one of those big cats for a pillow!

What a mighty God we serve. God delivered Daniel! He kept him safe. He brought him through the lion's den untouched. He lifted him out of that dark dungeon and back into the light of day! He restored him to favor with the king!

The sixth chapter of Daniel goes on to tell how the king rounded up all of Daniel's enemies and threw them into the lion's den. This time the lion's jaws were not shut up by an angel. They destroyed and devoured their prey. The weapon that was formed against Daniel destroyed the people who formed it!

DON'T STOP WITNESSING

WHY DOES the devil form weapons against God's people? Why does he attack us? Why does he cause trouble, pain, confusion, and calamity? Why did he want Daniel in the lions' den? Why did he want Shadrach, Meshach, and Abednego thrown into a fiery furnace?

Here's a bottom line truth you don't want to miss! Satan forms weapons against God's people *to shut them up!*

Daniel was the only one praying and being faithful to God in his neighborhood. Out of thousands of Jews in Babylon, Shadrach, Meshach, and Abednego were the only ones who wouldn't bow down to Nebuchadnezzar's golden idol. They were the only witnesses of God's goodness and God's grace. The devil said, "If I can shut them up, I can stop people from being influenced for Jehovah."

But God said, "NO! No weapon formed against My servants shall prosper! No scheme the devil devises against those who are serving Me will succeed."

So when hardship comes, don't panic. Hold onto your faith. When trial and suffering come across your path, don't think God has forsaken you. The devil just wants to discourage you, shut you down, and stop your witness for Christ. That's all it is! He can never defeat you if you hold on and stay true.

I know how to come against that lying devil. I take my Bible in hand, and I say, "Mr. Devil, you sit over here and let me preach to you. There's nobody here except you and me and the Lord. I know you think I don't know what I'm talking about, but you'd better pay some attention.

"Mr. Devil, the weapon that you formed against me doesn't mean much to me! I've read in God's Word that just one angel can take care of anything you stir up. One single angel is going to come down from heaven and bind you. You're going to fall, Devil. You're going to be cast into the bottomless pit for a thousand years. Then just for a little while you'll be turned loose to stir up the nations and wage war against God. Then you're history—you're going to be defeated and will burn in the lake of fire forever.

"You can run around accusing and afflicting for a little while longer, Mr. Devil. But I have a word for you right out of the Bible. We can call it your eulogy! Listen to me, now. The Word says, 'At the name of Jesus every knee should bow, of things in heaven, and things in earth, and things under the earth; and that every tongue should confess that Jesus Christ is Lord, to the glory of God the Father' (Phil. 2:10–11)."

Hallelujah!

CHAPTER SIX

FAITH TO OVERCOME

I S YOUR FAITH taking you someplace? Or do you feel as if you were on the road to nowhere? Maybe your job is a dead end . . . or you wish you were married but can't find the right person . . . or you're just tired of the way you're living your life.

Are you living in poverty and need, frustrated by unfulfilled ambitions? Are you tormented by worry, fear, and the cares of this life? Is your heart dead and cold toward God?

If so, your faith needs to be reactivated. Don't forget that faith is the victory that overcomes the world. (See 1 John 5:4.)

Your faith in God can take you farther than any motivational program or self-help book. Faith in God—faith that is going someplace—is your key to unlocking some positive changes in your life.

First of all, realize that God wants your life to be happy and victorious. *The MESSAGE* version of 3 John 2 says, "I pray for good fortune in everything you do, and for your good health—that your everyday affairs prosper, as well as your soul." The psalmist declared, "Commit thy way unto the Lord; trust also in him; and he shall bring it to pass" (Ps. 37:5).

Commit! There's a word for you. The Latin root of this word means "to connect, entrust." You have to make a connection with God, then entrust your way to Him. Turn over your interests, your activities, your concerns, your everything to God. Do you trust Him to know what is best for you and to bring it to pass? Or are you trying to work everything out for yourself?

TRUST GOD ENOUGH TO SERVE HIM HIS WAY

I'M SURE you have memorized Romans 8:28—"And we know that all things work together for good to them that love God, to them who are the called according to his purpose."

Do you love Him? Is your primary desire, your life's mission, to carry out God's purpose—to do His will? Is what God wants for you more important than what you think you want for yourself?

When you love God—truly love Him—you will find that His stuff is more important to you than your stuff. Doing what He wants you to do is more important than having your own way. Love is not passive— it is not just lip service. Love gets involved. Love takes a stand for what is right. Love refuses to compromise.

The service that results from love is not slavery. It is not forced. It is a natural outgrowth of the *relationship* between God and man. When you're loving and serving God, you know that you're never out of the watchful eye of the Lord. Living in relationship with the Lord means walking close to Him all the time, in sunshine and shadow, in good times and bad, in laughter and tears. Your life is consistent, the same, unchanging. You love God, relate to Him, serve Him every day, in every way, whatever comes. You don't do your own thing, go your own way, and then call on God to rescue you when you get into trouble. You serve Him all the time, and depend on Him to meet your needs and take care of you.

In Luke, chapter 15, Jesus told a powerful story about the prodigal son who demanded that his father give him his inheritance at once. He took his share and went into a far country, wasting everything on riotous living. When he'd spent all his money, and his good-time friends had abandoned him, the son ended up slopping the hogs for a farmer. He even found himself eating with the pigs.

Then the son "came to himself" (v. 17). He said, "Even the servants in my father's house live far better than me—they have a roof over their heads, and clothing to wear, and food to eat. I'll go back to my father and beg his forgiveness. Maybe he'll let me be a servant." (See Luke 15:17–19.)

What are you asking God for? Are you demanding that He give you what belongs to you, your rightful share, or are you asking Him to let you be His servant? Have you wasted your resources and opportunities on worldly pleasures, or on the pursuit of self-centered plans and dreams?

Jesus said, "Ask, and it shall be given you; seek, and ye shall find; knock, and it shall be opened unto you" (Luke 11:9).

You can have what you want, but you may not want what you get! The psalmist recalled the experience of the Israelites who forgot what God had done for them and His plan for them. Instead, they "lusted exceedingly in the wilderness, and tempted God in the desert. And he gave them their request; but sent leanness unto their soul" (Ps. 106:14–15).

The Lord said, "What things soever ye desire, when ye pray, believe that ye receive them, and ye shall have them" (Mark 11:24).

Don't pray until you know that your desire is in the

will of God for you. *The MESSAGE* translates the same verse like this—"I urge you to pray for absolutely everything, ranging from small to large. Include everything as you embrace this God-life, and you'll get God's everything."

I heard about a young man who said he didn't want to become a Christian because he wouldn't be able to continue doing the things he wanted to do. "Sure, you can," said the Christian friend who was witnessing to him. "But when God saves you, He changes you so you don't want to do the things you used to do!"

When you love God, serve God, and have a daily relationship with God, He gives you faith to say to the world's system—to materialism, popularity, fame, and the gods of this world—"I will not bow to you. I will not be deceived by you. Take this whole world, but give me Jesus!"

The Bible says, "Love not the world, neither the things that are in the world . . . for all that is in the world, the lust of the flesh, and the lust of the eyes, and the pride of life, is not of the Father, but is of the world. And the world passeth away, and the lust thereof: but he that doeth the will of God abideth for ever" (1 John 2:15–17). The things of the world cry for our attention. But they are fleeting things, temporary pleasures . . . here for a moment and then gone. Only what is done for the true and living God will last.

What can compare to the God we serve? He is the

God who possesses heaven and earth. He is the God who was Abraham's exceedingly great reward. He is the God of Isaac and the God of Rehoboth, who makes room for us. He is the God of Jacob, the God who wrestled all night with him. He is the God of Israel, the God with whom Moses spoke face to face. He is the God who heard the prayer of Joshua and made the earth stand still. He is the God of David, the sweet psalmist of Israel, who strengthened and empowered him to kill a lion, a bear, and a giant warrior named Goliath.

He is the God we can depend on, the God we can serve through good times and bad, the God who overcomes. Jesus said, "In the world, ye shall have tribulation: but be of good cheer; I have overcome the world" (John 16:33).

Pray . . . and Wait on God

Do you want to be an overcomer? How do you build that kind of relationship with God? It cannot be accomplished in one hour on Sunday morning. You have to make time to spend with the Lord daily. You must give God an opportunity to draw close to you. Prayer is a two-way exchange—have to have some long conversations with Him. Too many people get on their knees, say all the things that are on their minds, then get up and leave! How could they hear from heaven if they were already up and gone when the Lord replied?

If you're going to build a relationship with God, you must learn to pray. And to pray successfully, you must wait on God. The Lord said to Moses, "Come up on this mountain; I want to speak to you," so Moses made the climb. When he got there, he heard nothing. He didn't hear God's voice the next day either, or the next. Finally on the seventh day, the scriptures say that God spoke to him. (See Exodus 24:12–16.)

If Moses had left after three days . . . or after six, he would have missed God. He sat up there a week before the Lord spoke. Today, too many people can't stay on their knees before God for ten minutes!

"But they that wait upon the Lord shall renew their strength; they shall mount up with wings as eagles; they shall run, and not be weary; and they shall walk, and not faint" (Isa. 40:31). Wait on the Lord—minister to Him. When you do, you get His strength in exchange for your weakness.

There's another kind of wait—when you're waiting for His direction. If you will ask Him and wait for Him, He will order your steps and direct your path.

Maybe your world is filled with strife and discord, hectic goings and comings, even anger and violence. In the words of Shakespeare, it is "a tale told by an idiot, full of sound and fury, signifying nothing."* The Bible says, "Thou wilt keep him in perfect peace, whose mind is stayed on thee: because he trusteth in thee"

---

* Shakespeare, "Macbeth", Act V, Scene V.

(Isa. 26:3) Where is your mind? Is it scattered, confused, troubled? It must be "stayed"—stopped, parked, focused, concentrated. On what? On God.

The World's Peace—Or God's Peace?

Jesus said, "Peace I leave with you, my peace I give unto you: not as the world giveth, give I unto you. Let not your heart be troubled, neither let it be afraid" (John 14:27). What is the difference between worldly peace and Christ's peace? In the world, peace means a cessation of hostilities, a quieting down of noise and strife. Christ's peace is much more—the cure for troubled minds and fearful hearts.

I heard about an art contest that was held for the best depiction of peace. Many talented artists submitted works to the judges, and although created in different styles and media, most of the entries followed a similar theme. There was a beautiful drawing of a mother holding a newborn baby to her breast. There was a painting of a herd of cattle standing in a meadow, contentedly grazing beneath a sunlit sky. A sculptor had fashioned a plowshare from the twisted metal of a sword. But none of these works of art won the prize. What was the winner?

It was a huge canvas that skillfully captured a violent storm sweeping in from the sea. The sky was darkened by angry clouds, ripped apart with jagged, menacing streaks of lightning. Angry waves with boiling white-caps crashed upon the rugged, rocky shore. And at first no one could understand how such a frightening scene was supposed to depict peace. Upon closer examination, they saw a tiny nest in the cleft of a rock on the edge of a cliff. Inside that shelter, a little bird was sleeping, head tucked under its wing.

That is the kind of peace Christ provides—a peace that passes all understanding, a shelter in the time of storm.

You can have faith to overcome. How can you be victorious? "Casting all your care upon him; for he careth for you" (1 Pet. 5:7). As you spend time with God and develop a relationship with Christ Jesus, you will discover that "we have not an high priest which cannot be touched with the feeling of our infirmities; but was in all points tempted like as we are, yet without sin" (Heb. 4:15). The Lord understands just what you're going through. He's already been down that road and been faced with the same trials and testings that you're facing. He feels your pain, and He cares. Best of all, He wants you to know there is a way out—a victorious way.

DON'T LET THE PURPOSE OF MAN OVERRIDE THE PURPOSE OF GOD

ONE OF the most colorful characters in all of the Bible

is the man God chose to provide the name for His chosen people. His name is Israel. But that wasn't his name to begin with.

Genesis 25 tells his story. The Bible says that after Isaac's bride, Rebecca, conceived, a war began in her womb. She sought the Lord about this, and He told her there were two nations inside her that would be headed by the twin sons she would bear. Each child represented a nation. The turmoil she sensed inside would ultimately result in a reversal of the natural order of things. God said, "The elder shall serve the younger" (Gen. 25:23).

According to custom and tradition, the firstborn son was the natural heir to the priesthood of the family and was to receive a double portion of the father's inheritance. But in the case of the sons born to Isaac, the jostling for position and contention for power began even before birth. Esau was the natural heir, but even in the womb Jacob was scheming and wrestling, trying to get out first.

Esau was the firstborn, but Jacob emerged right behind him, holding onto his brother's heel. Throughout his growing-up years he was constantly competing with his brother, trying to take unfair advantage.

That's how he stole his brother's birthright. When Esau came in from the field faint with hunger, Jacob said, "I'll give you something to eat if you'll give me your birthright." (See Genesis 25:31.)

"What good is it to me if I die of hunger and thirst?" said Esau, and agreed to Jacob's sneaky deal. Not believing that his brother would hold him to such an unreasonable bargain, Esau was tricked.

Next Jacob tricked his father, Isaac (whose eyes were too weak and dim to notice that Jacob had covered his smooth arms with animal fur), into believing that he was Esau, who was a strong, outdoorsy man, with much body hair. Isaac pronounced the blessing that would have gone to Esau upon Jacob. (See Genesis 27.) Even though Jacob had lied and deceived his father, once the inheritance blessing was bestowed upon him, it could never be given to Esau.

Later, Jacob went to live with his uncle, Laban, to avoid ongoing conflict with Esau. Even while he lived with Laban, marrying two of Laban's daughters, Jacob schemed and connived to take financial advantage of him. By the time Laban caught onto Jacob's scheme, Jacob had made himself a wealthy man, with great riches and possessions. But he'd also worn out his welcome and was forced to move back to his homeland.

Jacob's deceptions began to catch up to him. He had cheated his father and brother and had to leave home. Then he cheated his uncle, and in getting away from his uncle was forced to go back to face his brother. Ah, but Jacob always had a new scheme going. Hearing that his brother would have an armed and hostile "welcome party" waiting for him, he put together a large peace offering and sent it on ahead. Then he divided his wives and possessions and sent them ahead of him, throwing them upon the mercy of Esau's court in an attempt to appease his brother's anger.

After a while, everybody was gone except Jacob. He had escaped from Laban. He had avoided having to face Esau. He had manipulated everybody and worked another scam. He almost got away with it. But he could not con God.

When Jacob was alone one night, a heavenly wrestler showed up and began to grapple with him. Jacob had believed himself to be a champion wrestler—after all, he'd been wrestling with somebody from the time he was in his mother's womb. He fought with this new adversary, pushing, twisting, struggling, trying to overcome. But he could not overcome.

The wrestling continued all night, back and forth, give and take, up and down. At daybreak the battle still wasn't over. The Bible says of the heavenly wrestler, "When he saw that he prevailed not against him, he touched the hollow of [Jacob's] thigh; and the hollow of Jacob's thigh was out of joint, as he wrestled with him" (Gen. 32:25).

"Let me go; it's getting daylight," said the visitor.

But Jacob said, "I will not let thee go, except thou bless me" (v. 26).

So the wrestler asked, "What is your name?" And Jacob told him. Then the heavenly being said, "You shall no longer be called Jacob, but Israel, because as a prince you have power with God and with men." (See Genesis 32:27–28.)

Although much of Jacob's behavior was not admirable, one cannot help but be impressed by his tenacity—by his determination to hold on until he received something from God. Too often when trying to find the will and purpose of God in our lives, we wrestle until we see the least little bit of daylight, then we're gone. We don't stay until God completes the work. As soon as we think we can get away, we take off. If we can work out a scheme, we're gone. If we can gain some momentary advantage, we're through. But we never see our confrontation with God through to a satisfactory conclusion.

But Jacob did. And he received the tremendous news that, as a prince, he had favor with God and men.

On the other hand, it appears that Jacob's "tenacity" was probably more sheer stubbornness than anything. The truth is he received the blessing, but not because he was a fierce wrestler . . . not because he was a schemer and manipulator, a deceiver and smart operator. In fact, Jacob had been wrestling need-lessly . . . in vain. He had been in encounters with Esau and Isaac, and with Laban, and now a confrontation with God . . . to no avail.

All that happened to Jacob had been foretold by God at the time of Jacob's birth. God had said it would come to pass. Jacob didn't need to try and make it happen. All he had to do was serve God and wait for His word to be fulfilled!

God's will is going to come to pass in your life. All you have to do is seek the Lord and walk close to Him. The Holy Ghost has come to lead and guide you, to empower and enable you, to energize you. The Helper has come alongside to bring you into fellowship with God, to anoint your ears to hear, your eyes to see, and to cause your heart to open and receive what God has prepared for you.

Don't try to make it happen. Don't let your plans and program override the purpose of God for your life. Let God bring His word and His will to pass. He wants to bless you and make you an overcomer.

Opportunity . . . and Opposition

One day I was listening to a local radio news station and heard a report that the Detroit Board of Education was going to sell some surplus school property. Our church had been believing God for a school for about ten years, so I was immediately interested. When I got back to the office, I had a secretary call for more information, such as what schools were going to be available and where they were located.

Most of the properties were too small for our needs or were not in a suitable location. All except one—

a huge facility in the heart of Detroit's inner city. I made arrangements with a realtor to look at it. The building had 179,000 square feet of floor space and sat on seven-and-a-half acres of land, with parking for seven hundred cars. It had not been designed as a public school, but had once housed a large Baptist church that had moved out of the inner city and built a new building in the suburbs.

Somehow the school system had acquired the property, but never used it. The building sat empty for years, and was in an advanced stage of deterioration. But the original architectural design was excellent, and I could see that the structure still had enormous potential.

"How much is the board asking for this property?" I asked the realtor.

He said it had been listed for about a half million dollars.

"Amazing," I said, "that's less than we paid for our present building." I put in a bid for the building that same day.

Two weeks later I received a copy of a letter from the Board of Education to all the parties that had looked at the building or made offers, notifying them of our offer and disclosing the amount of our bid. By this time my congregational leaders had approved the purchase and secured a loan commitment from our bank. I immediately phoned the Board's housing department and complained, "You can't shop my bid around to all your other prospects. That's unlawful. If you continue to do this, I'm going to sue you."

Unbeknown to me, the facility had been promised to a political group that had been expecting to get the property as a gift, for a one-dollar contract. My bid on behalf of our church messed up the plan. The board couldn't very well give away a property we were willing to pay for.

The next day a campaign of outrageous charges and personal attacks against me was launched. Rumors started circulating that the church seeking to buy the property was pastored by a guy named Merritt, who obviously was a drug dealer and a money launderer. "The school system should not be dealing with this kind of person," people said.

To make matters worse, about the same time this attack began, an angry and confused man began picketing in the street outside our church every Sunday morning, carrying a large, double-faced sign. One side read, "Pastor Is Not of God," the other side read, "Tithing Is Not of God." He was not breaking any law, and there was no way to make him quit. He attracted much attention and got quite a bit of publicity. It was a nightmare for me.

We'd received some rough, preliminary estimates that the cost of refurbishing the property would be approximately six million dollars. That seemed like an astronomical amount of money, but we also discovered that the replacement value of the finished project would be nearly thirty million dollars—five times what we would have invested.

Even so, the sheer size of the project caused some of the congregation to be confused and fearful. One of my acquaintances, a Jewish businessman whose knowledge and experience I respected, told me I was crazy to even consider investing six million dollars in Detroit's inner city. "That's like pouring money down the drain," he said.

A man in our church who was a millionaire and a former NFL football player, felt that our congregation should get out of the inner-city ghetto's mean streets and move to the suburbs. "You don't need this kind of harassment, Pastor. Forget the whole project. If we're going to spend that kind of money, let's go look for some land in a better location."

Yet, in my heart I felt strongly that God wanted our church to stay in the inner city. The people there—the poor, the downtrodden, the outcasts of today's society—were those to whom our church was supposed to be ministering. With virtually no other churches in the heart of the city remaining open for services on Sunday night—or any other night—because of fear of the gangs, crack dealers, and drive-by shootings, I felt somebody should take a stand and proclaim the power of the gospel. If our faith wouldn't work there, what good was it in the suburbs?

One day I learned that there had been a break-in at the abandoned building we were trying to buy, and vandals had done a great deal more damage. So I went back to the school board and renegotiated our sales offer down to $250,000—half of our previous bid. But there were still some areas of disagreement, and a mountain of red tape to be sorted out, before we would have a doable deal.

Eventually I caved in to the pressure and the conflict. Every day the radio station was calling me a drug dealer and money launderer. The Sunday morning demonstrator was still going strong, coming up with new and equally outrageous signs every few weeks to get more publicity. And my ex-football player friend still wanted to buy land in the suburbs.

I rode with him out to the suburbs several times, and we found a nice eight-acre lot near a safe residential area. My friend personally signed a real estate offer to buy it. So now we had options on two locations—one in the downtown area and one out of the city. What would we do? What should we do?

Finally I couldn't take any more. I cleared my schedule and ran for cover. I took my family on a week's vacation to New Orleans. I wanted to get away and not think about all the problems. I had reservations in a nice hotel, but it was packed and jammed, as was the whole city. On top of that, it rained for several days, which ruined the pleasure of sightseeing, shopping, going to eat—anything we wanted to do. Everybody was frustrated.

A GUIDING WORD FROM GOD

BY FRIDAY of that miserable week, I was totally disgusted. As I knelt to pray in my personal devotional time, the Lord spoke to me and said, "Son, I didn't call you to run; I gave you faith to overcome!"

"What's that, Lord?"

"I didn't call you to run; I gave you the faith to overcome!"

As I sought God's guidance and direction, a plan of action began to form in my mind. I felt that I finally knew the will of God and the steps that should be taken to work out the problems.

When I called my contact at the Board of Education, he was glad to hear from me. "Pastor Merritt, if you'll be in my office on Monday at 2:00 P.M., we can straighten out all the problems and, by the time you leave, we'll have a deal." I agreed to meet him.

By the time we were through on Monday, we had cut through all the red tape and had a final sales contract for the entire property . . . for $155,000. The only remaining technicality was to get formal approval at the next school board meeting.

That, as could be expected, did not go well. As soon as the meeting was called to order, one of the members spoke up saying, "I have a problem with one of the agenda items. I'm telling you right now that I don't want to even hear anyone mention Straight Gate [the name of our church], period. I don't want to vote on this deal. It still needs discussion. Let's table the matter." And they did.

After the meeting, I went over and introduced myself to the woman who so strongly opposed voting to approve the sale. I soon found out why she was so upset. She told me about the terrible suffering of her sick child. "Where was God when my daughter needed help?" she demanded. "Why should I do anything for any church?"

"I can't answer your question," I replied. "All I can say is that I believe God does care about your daughter. He loves you and wants to meet your needs. And, first of all, He wants to be your friend and bring peace to your soul."

The woman kept trying to fuss with me, and I politely, but firmly, refused to take the bait. I witnessed to her as best I could, and assured her that I would pray for her and her family. Then I left.

For the next two weeks I prayed earnestly every day about the building project, about the school board member and her daughter, and about all the other ongoing problems and difficulties. I refused to get discouraged or to try to carry all the burden on my own shoulders.

"Lord, I just want Your will to be done," I prayed. I felt a sense of peace about it.

At the next Board of Education meeting, the superintendent called the meeting to order and said, "I need a motion to sell this building to . . . "

Before he finished his sentence, the lady who had opposed the project two weeks earlier said, "I move that we sell the building to Straight Gate Church according to the terms of the proposed contract." There was no discussion, and fifteen seconds later all the members had voted "aye." It was a done deal.

At this writing, Straight Gate Church now occupies the property we bought that night. It has been completely remodeled and refurbished, with a state-of-the-art television production center, at a cost of six million dollars. Only about a third of that remains to be paid.

Ours is now a thriving church with a membership of some six thousand members. We average about twenty-five hundred people in our Sunday morning service. And, yes, we do have a service on Sunday night and at least one during the midweek as well. We are not afraid. Our doors are open. Anyone is welcome to come in and hear the truth about God. Every week hundreds of people are being saved, delivered, healed, filled with the Holy Spirit, and built up in their faith.

We are living proof that the faith God gives is faith to overcome.

Your faith can make you an overcomer. God is at

work. He is interested in everything that concerns and touches you. He will never leave you nor forsake you. He can—and often does—alter circumstances, solve problems, send the people and provisions you need into your life, comfort your sorrows, encourage and energize you, and make you successful and happy in all that you do.

God is saying, "Have I got a deal for you!" It never fails. You can't lose. "He that overcometh shall inherit all things; and I will be his God, and he shall be my son" (Rev. 21:7).

That's where your faith is taking you.

CHAPTER SEVEN

YOUR FAITH
WON'T FAIL YOU

FAITH IS the most powerful force in the universe. We humans seldom comprehend just how strong faith really is. Only a handful of people ever commit themselves to a level of dedication—totally sold out to God—where they experience the ultimate level of faith in this world.

This *super faith,* if you will, brings a person to the place where he can dwell in the presence of God and have fellowship with Him on a continuous basis. When this happens, that person actually lives in God's glory—here and now, on this earth.

Moses was one of the rare individuals who reached

the point where, through faith, he walked so close to God that he literally lived in His presence. The Bible says, "And the Lord spake unto Moses face to face, as a man speaketh unto his friend" (Exod. 33:11). Moses lived in God's glory and communed with Him, receiving direction and instruction from God that continues to be a guide and a law to mankind to this very day.

On those occasions when Moses would come out from the presence of God to speak to the people, he was enveloped in divine glory. His countenance glowed with a supernatural light. "And the children of Israel saw the face of Moses, that the skin of Moses' face shone" (Exod. 34:35). The Bible says Moses actually put on a veil so Aaron and the people could look upon him.

What had happened? I believe the physical Moses had already *died,* had literally already ceased to exist in the common, earthly form. His body had already been changed by the unimaginable, immeasurable power of the glory of God.

You say, "But Moses died later on." And I suggest to you that when death presented itself to Moses, it was swallowed up in victory. It was not the ordinary event common to mankind. Death had no sting. The grave had no triumph. The Word says, "So Moses the servant of the Lord died there in the land of Moab, according to the word of the Lord. And he buried him in a valley in the land of Moab . . . but no man knoweth of his sepulcher unto this day" (Deut. 34:5–6).

Why in the world would the grave of such a great leader as Moses be unmarked and unknown? Surely the people of Israel would have built a monument there, and made his tomb a national shrine. Why didn't this happen? Because God did not leave his body there! The Bible speaks of the archangel Michael contending with the devil for the body of Moses, to take it into heaven. (See Jude 1:9.)

Moses is not the only example of a man who achieved such a high level of faith that he overcame the power of death. The Old Testament tells us of a man named Enoch who had a very special relationship with the Almighty. We know that he existed, for there is a record of his sons and daughters. He was the father of Methuselah, who at age 969 apparently was the world's oldest man. I don't know what else was so notable about Enoch that the Lord regarded him as so special. Hebrews 11 tells us that "he had this testimony, that he pleased God" . . . and "without faith it is impossible to please him" (vv. 5–6). It must have been his faith and his desire to dwell in the presence and the glory of God that overcame the power of death. The Bible says, "And Enoch walked with God: and he was not; for God took him" (Gen. 5:24).

Elisha was a mighty prophet of God, the man who received a double portion of the spirit of Elijah. The Scriptures record that God performed twice as many miracles through his ministry as Elijah had seen. Elisha certainly was one of those rare individuals whose faith took him someplace—from the earthly realm into the spiritual. He heard the voice of God speaking. He saw the hand of God at work.

How do I know this? The Bible tells how the king of Syria tried to capture Elisha to keep him from prophesying to the king of Israel about what the Syrians were plotting against the Jews. He sent a great army to Dothan where Elisha was staying, with chariots and horses, with a great host of soldiers. They marched in by night and totally surrounded the city.

The next morning Elisha's servant got up and looked out the window. He was distressed—terrorized—to see this great army. He ran to tell his master, and asked, "What are we going to do?"

"Relax!" said Elisha. "Fear not: for they that be with us are more than they that be with them" (2 Kings 6:16).

I think Elisha's servant tried to believe. He wanted to be assured. But everywhere he looked there was a multitude of armed soldiers with the latest and most powerful weapons of war, all pointed toward Elisha's house. And he kept trembling in anxiety.

Why wasn't Elisha worried? Because he walked in the presence of God and was already living in the glory of the Lord. He knew the mind and the will of God. He could see what no one else could see. But understanding his servant's distress, "Elisha prayed, and said,

140

Lord, I pray thee, open his eyes, that he may see. And the Lord opened the eyes of the young man; and he saw: and, behold, the mountain was full of horses and chariots of fire round about Elisha" (2 Kings 6:17). I believe God's heavenly army outnumbered the Syrians a hundred to one! Without any struggle at all, Elisha and his servant were delivered from the enemy.

The New Testament gives a report of the ministry of an evangelist named Philip, who preached Christ and did many wonders and miracles among the people. He conducted a great revival in the city of Samaria, and an abundant harvest of souls were saved. The Bible says, "And there was great joy in that city" (Acts 8:8).

Right in the middle of this great citywide crusade, the angel of the Lord gave Philip a message to leave the revival and go out into the desert where there was nobody. Philip went. It may have seemed as if he were on the road to nowhere, but I believe he realized that his faith was taking him someplace! And sure enough, when he got to the road that runs from Jerusalem to Gaza, a chariot came rolling through the desert carrying the servant of the queen of Ethiopia. The Spirit sent Philip over to minister to that man, who was hungry for God. Philip explained the Scriptures and preached Jesus to him. Then, as the chariot came upon an oasis where there was a pool of water, Philip baptized the Ethiopian upon his profession of faith in the Lord Jesus Christ. Tradition says this man went back to

Ethiopia as a missionary, preaching the gospel to his own people.

But I want you to notice something remarkable. There's no record of anything like this anywhere else in the Bible. "And when they were come up out of the water, the Spirit of the Lord caught away Philip, that the eunuch saw him no more: and he went on his way rejoicing. But Philip was found at Azotus" (Acts 8:39–40).

How did Philip travel from the desert all the way to Azotus, many miles away? His faith took him there! The Spirit of the Lord, with whom Philip dwelled, caused his body to disregard the limitations of the flesh and instantly to be transported a great distance that would ordinarily have taken several days to travel.

When we are living by faith, using our faith, moving with our faith, letting our faith take us someplace, I believe we will reach a level where there are no limitations. Nothing will be impossible to us. When we are working for the Lord, doing His will, we have unlimited power at our disposal. Jesus said, "All power is given unto me in heaven and in earth . . . and, lo, I am with you always, even unto the end of the world" (Matt. 28:18, 20).

Christ wants to bring us to the point of realization that nothing can defeat us or overpower us. He wants us to receive the revelation that we can be surrounded by His presence, endued with His power, saturated with His glory. At that point, we die to ourselves and all human limitations. The apostle Paul discovered this, and proclaimed, "I am crucified with Christ: nevertheless I live; yet not I, but Christ liveth in me: and the life which I now live in the flesh I live by the faith of the Son of God, who loved me, and gave himself for me" (Gal. 2:20).

The greatest miracle that can ever happen to a person is salvation. And the next greatest miracle is the miraculous step into God's glory, which is the ultimate destination of faith that is going someplace. This faith triumphs over everything. Nothing can defeat it—not persecution, suffering, pain, or death. You see, death claims no child of God. The process of being born again shortcircuits the power of death. Jesus said, "Whosoever liveth and believeth in me shall never die" (John 11:26). What happens at the end of our earthly existence is not death, but rest. Revelation 14:13 says, "Blessed are the dead which die in the Lord from henceforth: Yea, saith the Spirit, that they may rest from their labors; and their works do follow them."

Your faith is taking you someplace. It will not fail you. And you will discover that what others call death is merely a stepping stone from this world into the eternal presence and glory of God. Here is a revolutionary truth that will change your whole outlook on life. Once you truly understand this, what could possibly happen on this earth to keep you from serving God.

The Lord said, "Fear not them which kill the body, but are not able to kill the soul" (Matt. 10:28). The Bible provides many amazing examples of this powerful principle of faith.

Fiery Furnace Faith

ONE OF the most exciting examples is found in the Old Testament Book of Daniel. Shadrach, Meshach, and Abednego were young Hebrew princes who had been taken captive by Nebuchadnezzar, king of Babylon. They had been trained in his college, had excelled in their training, and been placed in responsible positions in the kingdom. Though they had found favor in Babylon, the three Hebrew children did not forget who they were and never failed to realize that they owed allegiance first to the Lord God Jehovah. They remembered the laws of God that commanded them to worship no other gods before Him, and not to bow to any idol or worship any graven image, for the Lord is a jealous God. (See Exodus 20.)

It came to pass that Nebuchadnezzar, who claimed to be a god, decided to create a huge golden image of himself in the middle of Babylon, nine feet wide and ninety feet high. He issued a decree that when the king's musicians played the royal fanfare, all the people, free and slave, were to bow down and worship the golden image. Anyone who failed to obey risked facing the king's wrath . . . and the punishment of death.

Shadrach, Meshach, and Abednego realized they were in a dilemma. God's law forbade them to bow down to any graven image or to worship any other god than Jehovah. Yet Nebuchadnezzar's law said that if they didn't worship his image, they would die. It was only a matter of time until they were faced with a choice of whose law to obey.

Sure enough, one day as they were going about their business, they heard the royal musicians play the king's fanfare. Immediately everybody stopped what they were doing and bowed down and worshiped Nebuchadnezzar's golden idol—all except the three young Jewish men.

Take notice that there were thousands of Jewish people in captivity in Babylon. All of them had been taught the laws of Moses from their childhood. Most of them recited the *Shema Yisrael* twice each day—"Hear, O Israel: The Lord our God is one Lord: and thou shalt love the Lord thy God with all thine heart, and with all thy soul, and with all thy might" (Deut. 6:4–5). They all knew that the Lord, the God of Abraham, Isaac, and Jacob, forcefully forbade idolatry and called himself a "jealous" God. Yet when they were put to the test, all of them—multiplied thousands, except three—caved in to the demands of Nebuchadnezzar.

"Well, we couldn't help it, we were slaves. We were powerless. We were at the mercy of the Persians. If we disobeyed, we'd have been executed. Then who would have looked after our children and taken care of the old people? We didn't have any choice but to do what the king demanded. Didn't you see that furnace, burning red hot? Surely God wouldn't expect us to obey His commands and risk being executed!"

But three of the Jews would not bow.

The word spread fast. "Shadrach, Meshach, and Abednego didn't bow down. They didn't worship the king's golden idol. What's going to happen to them now?"

The king's soldiers dragged the three young men through the streets to the palace and shoved them into the presence of a raging Nebuchadnezzar. "Is it true you disobeyed my royal decree and did not bow down to my gods and my image?"

It was true.

"Well, I'm going to give you one more chance. I'll have the musicians play the fanfare one more time just for you. If you fall down and worship as I have commanded, all will be well. But if you refuse, I'll burn you in the furnace! Think it over, boys. You have only one more chance to decide what you're going to do."

"Save yourself the trouble!" replied the three Hebrew princes. "We are not careful in answering you; we don't even have to think about it. We will not bow down. We will not compromise. If you throw us in the furnace, the God we serve is able to deliver us from your hand.

But if not, we still will not bow down and worship your image!" (See Daniel 3.)

Here is the key—*the God we serve!*. You have to *serve* God—work for Him and do His will. Every day Shadrach, Meshach, and Abednego pledged their love for God with all their heart, soul, mind, and strength. And because they loved Him, they served Him.

That's why they could be so sure that no weapon formed against them could prosper! Their deliverance was guaranteed, based upon their service.

These three served God all the time. So when the devil's weapon was formed against them, they didn't have to worry about it!

TAKE A STAND . . . REFUSE TO COMPROMISE

YOU HAVE to make up your mind to serve God, no matter what happens and no matter what others do. Decide that you will serve God when it is raining. You will serve Him when you are sick. You will serve Him when there isn't enough money to pay the bills and get by. You'll serve God when the kids are acting up. Make a commitment to serve God always, and do what He tells you to do.

Shadrach, Meshach, and Abednego served notice to King Nebuchadnezzar that they would serve God, never bowing to his idolatrous order. "We believe God will deliver us from any consequences you can devise," they said. "But if not, be it known unto thee, O king, that we will not serve thy gods, nor worship the golden image which thou has set up" (Dan. 3:18).

Be it known! Be it known to your backslidden husband. Be it known to your cold-hearted wife. Be it known to your rebellious children. Be it known to your employer, your banker, your neighbors. Be it known to you, prostitute. Be it known to you, drug dealer. Be it known to you, rap singer. Be it known to you, entertainment world. Be it known to you, popularity and fame. Be it known that we are not going to serve you, now or ever! Whatever happens, I will serve the Lord. I know He can deliver me from any harm or danger, but if not, I will still serve Him.

If God doesn't deliver me, it's not the end! There is another side of faith, and I am in God's hands. The apostle Paul wrote, "For whether we live, we live unto the Lord; and whether we die, we die unto the Lord: whether we live therefore, or die, we are the Lord's" (Rom. 14:8).

When Nebuchadnezzar heard the reply of the three Hebrew children, he went berserk with rage. He ordered his soldiers to bind Shadrach, Meshach, and Abednego, and to heat the furnace seven times hotter than it had ever been before. Then he commanded his mightiest men to throw the three rebellious Hebrews into the furnace. The Bible says that the furnace was so hot that when they opened the door, the heat rushed out and killed the soldiers who were shoving the victims inside.

When the doors were shut again, I can hear old Nebuchadnezzar speaking to the crowd that had gathered to watch the execution. "Let this be a lesson to you! Shadrach, Meshach, and Abednego were not delivered from the fire. Their God did not save them from my power. They should have bowed down to me!"

Then Nebuchadnezzar decided to take a peek inside the furnace to see if there was anything left of the men he had thrown inside to burn. Very carefully, he looked inside the opening to the fiery furnace—then jumped back in astonishment. "What's going on here?" he cried. "You were all witnesses! We threw three men, heavily bound, inside the furnace. But I just looked and there are four men in there, free and walking about. They are not burned or hurt at all. And the form of the fourth man is like the Son of God!" (See Daniel 3:24.)

Oh, what a testimony! What a miraculous report. Shadrach, Meshach, and Abednego loved God. They served Him. They had a relationship with Him. They had faith that wouldn't back down. And when the time of trial and crisis came, they refused to compromise their witness for the Lord. "God is able to deliver us," they said. "But if not, we still won't bow down to the world and the devil."

Here's the shocking part of the story. God *did not* deliver them from the trial of fire. He didn't! The three men were bound, tied up, put in shackles. They were made prisoners. Where was God? Why didn't He save them? Why didn't He keep them from the humiliation and pain?

Then things got worse. The furnace was heated seven times hotter than usual. It was so hot that just the heat coming out of the open door killed the strongest soldiers in Nebuchadnezzar's army. And the three persecuted children of God were thrown inside that deadly pit of fire!

They didn't escape the fire! They were thrown into the furnace. Their faith did not keep them from facing death at the hands of the executioners. Their faith was not a fire escape! They went into the fire, tied up, bound, enslaved.

What happened to Shadrach, Meshach, and Abednego? Where did their faith take them? What was the end result for them?

Into . . . and Through the Fire

Their faith did not keep them from the fire. It took them to the fire—and *into* the fire! Oh, but don't stop there! Their faith took them *through* the fire. Their faith gave them liberty in the midst of destruction. The ropes and chains that bound them were melted in the fervent heat—but their clothes didn't get scorched, and their hair wasn't even singed. Because they had loved God and served Him in the good times, Jesus Himself came to be with them and walk with them in the bad times!

Get this truth and never forget it! The three Hebrew children didn't get delivered; they got God! Their relationship with Him was not interrupted by anything man could do to them. In the fiery trial, they didn't receive superhuman strength or some secret weapon. God simply came to them and gave them more of Himself!

What did all of this ordeal accomplish? Now, don't miss the rest of the story. Nebuchadnezzar had the doors to the furnace opened, and he cried out, "Ye servants of the most high God, come forth." And in front of the king's princes, governors, captains, and counselors, with all the great multitude watching, Shadrach, Meshach, and Abednego walked out, unscathed, untouched, unharmed. Their ropes and chains were gone, and they walked out free. The fire had not hurt them. Their hair had not been singed. There was not even the smell of smoke on their clothes.

Then Nebuchadnezzar, the pagan king who wanted to be a god, proclaimed before that huge assembly of people, "Blessed be the God of Shadrach, Meshach, and Abednego, who hath sent his angel, and delivered his servants that trusted in him . . . Therefore I make a decree, That every people, nation, and language, which speak any thing amiss against the God of Shadrach, Meshach, and Abednego, shall be cut in pieces, and their houses shall be made a dunghill: because there is no other God that can deliver after this sort. Then the king promoted Shadrach, Meshach, and Abednego, in the province of Babylon" (Dan. 3:28–30).

God's Word will be proclaimed. His work will be carried out. The will of God will be done. His faith, placed in the hearts of people who will be faithful to serve Him, will produce results. And though the faith of God may not keep us from danger and trouble, it will bring us into the very presence of the Lord, and He will take us through the fiery ordeal. He will get us safely to the other side, to a place of blessing and honor and promotion! In the process, God will be glorified. His name will be praised in the midst of all the people.

Although the American church knows almost nothing about persecution, suffering for the cause of Christ is a reality in most other places in the world. And it is almost certain that the time will come in this country when religious freedom will cease and believers will be forced to make a choice—to renounce their faith or to take a stand for Christ. We will come to understand what the Lord meant when He said, "Think not that I am come to send peace on earth: I came not to send peace, but a sword . . . And he that taketh not his cross, and followeth after me, is not worthy of me. He that findeth his life shall lose it: and he that loseth his life for my sake shall find it" (Matt. 10:34, 38–39).

Make no mistake about it, your faith *will* be tried.

As soon as you set out to walk with Jesus, weapons will
be formed against you. "The disciple is not above his
master, nor the servant above his lord" (Matt. 10:24).

PETER'S TEST OF FAITH

WHEN SAUL of Tarsus, who had persecuted the early
church, had his dramatic confrontation with the Lord,
he was blinded by the light of God and knocked to the
ground. For the next three days his physical eyes were
blind but his spiritual eyes were being opened. He
prayed to the Lord, and God sent a disciple named
Ananias to pray for him that he might recover his sight.

Now, Ananias was reluctant to go near Saul (who
was to become Paul), knowing his reputation. "But the
Lord said unto him, Go thy way: for he is a chosen
vessel unto me, to bear my name before the Gentiles,
and kings, and the children of Israel: *for I will show him
how great things he must suffer for my name's sake*" (Acts
9:15–16, emphasis mine).

Most people today think of Paul as perhaps the
greatest disciple of all, a man of faith who traveled all
over the known world, preaching and witnessing before
kings, governors, and dignitaries, establishing churches,
and writing fourteen books of the New Testament. We
remember his tremendous accomplishments and are
blessed by the great wisdom of his writings. But what
about his sufferings? Hear his own testimony!

Are they ministers of Christ? . . . I am more; in labours more abundant, in stripes above measure, in prisons more frequent, in deaths oft. Of the Jews five times received I forty stripes save one. Thrice was I beaten with rods, once was I stoned, thrice I suffered shipwreck, a night and a day I have been in the deep; in journeyings often, in perils of waters, in perils of robbers, in perils by mine own countrymen, in perils by the heathen, in perils in the city, in perils in the wilderness, in perils in the sea, in perils among false brethren; in weariness and painfulness, in watchings often, in fastings often, in cold and nakedness. Besides those things that are without, that which cometh upon me daily, the care of all the churches.

—2 Corinthians 11:23–28

Can any of us compare our experiences of suffering with Paul's? I think not. Yet never did his faith waver.

The apostle Peter said, "If any man suffer as a Christian, let him not be ashamed; but let him glorify God" (1 Pet. 4:16). He also said, "Beloved, think it not strange concerning the fiery trial which is to try you, as though some strange thing happened unto you: but rejoice, inasmuch as ye are partakers of Christ's sufferings; that, when his glory shall be revealed, ye may be glad also with exceeding joy" (1 Pet. 4:12–13).

154

It is altogether fitting that Peter should be the one to write these stirring words, for he was perhaps the world's first wishy-washy Christian, up one minute . . . down the next. Peter was either bold and brash or cowardly and weak. He was either sharing brilliant spiritual insights . . . or missing the point altogether.

Jesus recognized Peter's tremendous potential and the spiritual battle going on inside him. He warned him that the devil was coming to try his faith. "And the Lord said, Simon, Simon, behold, Satan hath desired to have you, that he may sift you as wheat: but I have prayed for thee, that thy faith fail not" (Luke 22:31–32).

Peter said, "Lord, I'm doing fine. I'm ready to go anywhere with You—to prison, or even to death."

Then Jesus uttered the awful prophecy that is so well known even two thousand years later—"Before the cock crows today, you will deny Me three times." (See Luke 22:33–34.)

Watch out, Peter. Satan is after you!

One day when Jesus was again preparing His disciples for the coming events when He would be captured, tortured, and put to death on the cross, Peter jumped up and began to rebuke Jesus for saying such things—"Lord, these things shall not be!"

"But he turned, and said unto Peter, Get thee behind me, Satan: thou art an offence unto me: for thou savourest not the things that be of God, but those that be of men" (Matt. 16:23).

How's your faith holding up, Peter?

Then the fateful day arrived, and Jesus went to Gethsemane to agonize before the Father. He took the disciples with Him and asked them also to pray. When He checked on them a little later, they were asleep. "Simon, sleepest thou? couldest not thou watch one hour? Watch ye and pray, lest ye enter into temptation. The spirit truly is ready, but the flesh is weak" (Mark 14:37–38) Twice more the Lord returned to find the disciples sleeping.

Is your faith about to fail, Peter?

Soon the quietness of the garden was broken by the noise of marching feet and the glare of torches. Judas emerged from the shadows and gave Jesus the kiss of betrayal. Soldiers rushed in to arrest Jesus and his disciples. Peter rubbed the sleep from his eyes and prepared to fight off the intruders single-handedly. Grabbing his sword, he made a mighty swing and cut off the ear of the high priest's servant. Jesus ordered Peter to stop his resistance, and healed the stricken servant. Away the soldiers marched Jesus to the high priest's house to be charged. And Peter followed behind.

Careful, Peter, here comes the test! Will your faith fail?

We all know what happened next. Standing in the courtyard outside the court of Caiaphas, Peter fulfilled the prophecy of the Lord and denied three times that he was a disciple, or that he even knew Jesus. As the first rays of the coming dawn crept over the horizon, a rooster crowed. Startled, Peter looked up . . . and across the courtyard, Jesus turned His head and looked straight into his eyes.

Immediately Peter realized what he had done. And he went out and wept bitterly.

Where's your faith now, Peter? Where's all your cocky confidence? How could you do such a thing? Why didn't faith keep you from failing, from falling, from shame and disgrace? Where is your faith now that you feel so miserable, like a traitor to the One you claimed to love so much? It's over! You're through. What a failure!

Then they took Jesus out and crucified Him. On a rocky crag outside the city walls, He suffered, bled, and died. And Peter saw it happen . . . shivered in the eerie darkness . . . wept more bitter tears. Surely Satan had won. But with God, death is not the end, but the beginning!

Early on the following Sunday, a little group of women took spices and oil to anoint the body of the Savior. But the stone had been rolled away, and His tomb was empty. In their sorrowful confusion and despair, an angel spoke to them, reminding them that Jesus was risen just as He had told them He would. "Go your way, tell his disciples *and Peter* that he goeth before you into Galilee: there shall ye see him, as he said unto you" (Mark 16:7, emphasis added).

And Peter! Why would the angel make a point of mentioning his name? Here is a message from beyond the grave: *Peter, are you there? Is there still a glimmer of faith inside your breast? Do you remember the things He said to you? Have you forgotten that the Lord Himself prayed that your faith would not fail? Will you come back, Peter? Will you go to meet the Lord?*

Yes, Peter was there when the risen Christ appeared to His disciples—once, twice, three times. And on the day of that third meeting, Jesus said, "Simon, son of Jonas, lovest thou me?"

"Yes, Lord!"

"Feed my sheep."

Three times there was that amazing exchange. Three times Peter had denied the Lord, and three times he now proclaimed his renewed love and service. And Jesus said, "Follow me." (See John 21.)

Oh, Peter, Satan will not have you and sift you like wheat! Jesus' prayer has been answered. Your faith has not failed. Where will it take you now?

The Acts of the Apostles tells the story. From that day forward, wherever the Christian action was erupting in Jerusalem and the surrounding territories, Peter was in the thick of it. Preaching to multitudes, standing up to the doubters and enemies of Christ, expanding the scope of the early church, being a wise counselor and leader, standing stalwartly and unwaveringly—a rock! Tradition says that when Peter was old and opposition to the church rose in a fiery burst of persecution, he faced the challenge to be a martyr for

Christ. Threatened with crucifixion like his Lord had suffered, Peter said, "I am not worthy of such a death as His—hang me upside down!" And they did. But his faith did not fail, and soon Peter was with his blessed Lord.

The body of Christ needs to hear the truth today. What is the truth? God has given us faith, but faith has its price. Satan will come against us to test and try that faith. And in the trying of our faith, we are never exempt from pain, anguish, turmoil, and suffering. But our faith will not fail. The faith that God gives us will take us someplace, although it may well be someplace that in our natural minds we'd rather not go. Faith does not run from trouble; it will take you straight to the heart of danger, into the presence of your enemies, and through the valley of the shadow of death.

Jesus' faith took Him to Gethsemane . . . and Golgotha . . . to the cross.

John's faith took him into exile on the lonely Isle of Patmos, separated from his loved ones and his churches.

Peter's faith took him to an upside-down cross outside Jerusalem.

Paul's faith took him to Rome, to be beheaded on Nero's chopping block.

And Stephen's faith took him to a dusty road outside Jerusalem. His enemies bit him and tore his flesh. Then they stoned him. As the mob jeered and screamed, beating the life out of him with stones, Stephen's faith was still on the move, still taking him someplace.

Let me pause to remind you—Jesus' faith did not leave Him in the tomb. John's faith did not abandon him on Patmos. Peter's faith did not dead-end at an upside-down cross. And Paul's faith did not stop with a Roman execution. Oh, no, their faith took them *to* death, *through* death, and beyond!

Faith That Moved the Heart of God

Stephen's faith did not die in the dirt. Kneeling down, he prayed for his murderers, "Lord, lay not this sin to their charge" (Acts 7:60). You see, Stephen did not feel the fangs of hatred and the rocks of rage that tore him apart and mutilated his body. His earthly body may have been briefly aware of the pain, but not the real Stephen. His faith had already taken him someplace else! His eyes were looking into another world. And he was saying, "I see Jesus!"

Here's the good part! Don't miss this. "But he, being full of the Holy Ghost, looked up stedfastly into heaven, and saw the glory of God, and Jesus standing on the right hand of God" (Acts 7:55).

Standing! Jesus was standing? What's going on here? No less than three apostles—Mark (writing for Peter), Luke, and Paul, all refer to the glorified Son of God being *seated* at the right hand of God (see Mark 16:19; Luke 22:69; Eph. 1:20). Why would Stephen say he saw Jesus standing?

Because his faith had moved God! Jesus stood up to honor a faith that would not fail . . . and to welcome Stephen to heaven, into the joyous presence and unending glory of God.

ABOUT THE AUTHOR

ANDREW MERRITT is a thinker, a gifted expository teacher, and a passionate and powerful preacher. He holds both Bachelor's and Master's degrees in Theology.

With his wife, Viveca, he pastors the Straight Gate Church in Detroit, Michigan, which has a strong outreach to the inner city. Starting with only three members in 1979, Straight Gate Church now has some six thousand members, and has moved from six locations because of its phenomenal growth to its present seven-and-a-half-acre campus.

Pastor Merritt has been recognized as "Minister of the Year" by the Michigan Chapter of the Southern Christian Leadership Conference, and received the "YMCA Minority Achievers Award." He has been invited to give the invocation for the Michigan House of Representatives and at a session of the United States House of Representatives in Washington.

OTHER BOOKS BY MERRITT

The Marriage Enrichment Handbook
Pursue, Overtake, and Reclaim
Jesus Destroyed the Works of the Devil

For further information or for a list of available tapes, write to:

ANDREW MERRITT, PASTOR
STRAIGHT GATE CHURCH
10100 GRAND RIVER AVE., DETROIT, MI 48204-0389